The Feasts of the LORD
Study Guide

& Their Spiritual Significance in the Life of the Believer

© Copyright 2009 by Michael K. Lake, Th.D.
All Rights Reserved

BIBLICAL LIFE Publishing

P.O. Box 588 | Marshfield, MO 65706-0588
Phone: 417-859-0881 | Fax: 417-468-2037

The publishing arm of Biblical Life Assembly & Biblical Life College & Seminary

About the Teacher

Dr. Michael K. Lake
Chancellor and Founder, Biblical Life College & Seminary
Apostle/Bishop, Biblical Life Assembly

A.A. - United Theological Seminary ❖ Th.B. - Christian Bible College ❖ Th.M. - Christian Bible Seminary ❖ M.A. - Faith Theological Seminary ❖ Th.D. - North American School of Theology ❖ D.R.E. - New Covenant International Bible College ❖ D.Psy. - Faith Theological Seminary

Dr. Lake is the founder of BLCS and serves as an Educational Consultant for various Christian organizations around the world. He is ordained with the United Full Gospel Church and has served as Bishop for the denomination since 1999. Dr. Lake is listed in the U.S. Registry's "Who's Who Among Outstanding Americans," Sterling's "Who's Who Executive Edition" and the "Who's Who among American Teachers" for his accomplishments in ministry and with Biblical Life.

The Feasts of the LORD Study Guide | DVD

Bible Translations Used:

KJV – King James Bible. Public Domain.

TNK – JPS TANAKH 1985 (English). The TANAKH, a new translation (into contemporary English) of The Holy Scriptures according to the traditional Hebrew text (Masoretic). The Jewish Bible: Torah, Nevi'im, Kethuvim. Copyright © 1985 by The Jewish Publication Society. All rights reserved. This fresh translation began work in 1955. Used by permission.

AMP - Amplified Bible Copyright © 1954, 1958, 1962, 1964, 1965, 1987 by The Lockman Foundation, La Habra, CA 90631

CJB – Complete Jewish Bible. Copyright © 1998 by David H. Stern. Jewish New Testament Publications, Clarksville, MD 21029

Biblical Life Publishing

The Feasts of the LORD Study Guide | DVD

Table of Contents

Lessons	Page
Getting College Credit	5
Lesson One - Understanding Biblical Patterns	7
Lesson Two - The Basics of Understanding Babylon	27
Lesson Three - The Feasts of the LORD and Prophecy	45
Lesson Four - The Spring Feasts - Part 1	59
Lesson Five - The Spring Feasts - Part 2	70
Lesson Six - The Summer Feast	79
Lesson Seven - The Fall Feasts - Part 1	90
Lesson Eight - The Fall Feasts - Part 2	102
Lesson Nine - Hanukkah & Purim	114
Recommended Reading	124
Additional Resources	125

This study guide is designed to be used with the DVD set.

The Feasts of the LORD Study Guide | DVD

College Credit:

There are several ways that you can receive college credit for this seminar.

1. Local Bible Institute or School of Ministry

Biblical Life College & Seminary has teams with local bible institutes and schools of ministry around the world to allow students to receive college credit through the BLCS International Educational Network. If your local congregation has a school that is a member of the BLCS network, you can work with your school to receive credit through BLCS. All work and tuition should be submitted directly to your local school.

2. Biblical Life College & Seminary

If you do not have a local school that is a part of the BLCS International Educational Network, you can receive credit directly from BLCS. To receive credit for the seminar, please follow the directions below. Once all work is completed, mail in your work to BLCS along with tuition for 3 semester credit hours. The tuition is $160.00 for undergraduate credit. Make your check or money order payable to: Biblical Life.

Biblical Life Publishing

Biblical Life College & Seminary
ATTN: Fire Seminar
P.O. Box 588
Marshfield, MO 65706-0588

Instruction for Receiving College Credit

To gain three (3) semester credit hours for this seminar, you will need to:

1. Answer all review questions and assignments in this seminar workbook.

2. Find three books that cover some aspect dealt with in this study, read the books and develop a 5 to 10 page paper on each. Attention should be given to develop greater depth in personal application of the truths presented in the seminar.

3. Pick one topic within the scope of the study and develop a paper of 10 to 15 pages. Take time to share from your heart and look for the Holy Spirit to make certain subjects come alive to you as you study and write. We are not just looking for the amassing of facts, but we are seeking rhema that can be lived!

The Feasts of the LORD Study Guide | DVD

Lesson One

Understanding Biblical Patterns

For those of you who are new to studies at Biblical Life, our main goal is to return to a life that is completely biblical. We must carefully examine every concept, philosophy and tradition to ensure that they line up with the written, inspired Word of God. Those that do not line up with the Word must be graciously discarded by the serious believer. The Prophet Jeremiah, I believe, prophesied about believers doing just that as they approached the end of days:

> **Jeremiah 16:19 (NKJV)**
> ^{19} O Lord, my strength and my fortress, My refuge in the day of affliction, The Gentiles shall come to You From the ends of the earth and say, "Surely our fathers have inherited lies, Worthlessness and unprofitable *things.*"

<u>Manmade traditions keep believers in bondage and from fulfilling their destinies in Messiah</u>.

As we proceed with examining our traditions and embracing our Hebraic heritage, we must also examine Jewish traditions as well. Jesus warns us about extra-biblical traditions among the Jewish people:

> **Mark 7:13 (NKJV)**
> ^{13} making the word of God of no effect through your

Biblical Life Publishing

tradition which you have handed down. And many such things you do."

The truth of the matter is that both Christians and Jews, over the centuries, have added traditions to the Word of God that frustrate God's work in the earth. Everything, whether Christian or Jewish, must be diligently examined in light of the Word of God. The Apostle Paul challenges us to:

> **1 Thessalonians 5:21 (AMP)**
> ^{21} But test *and* prove all things [until you can recognize] what is good; [to that] hold fast.

A return to biblicity is a return to the ways of God, the blessings of God and the power of God. It is our conviction that for the days ahead the believer must walk in all three to fulfill their destiny in Messiah.

In the Beginning & Sanctification

When God created the heavens and the earth, He set things in motion to line up with the Kingdom of God. We will find later in this study that a second kingdom was established called Babylon. The Babylonian system is constantly warring against God's ways, timing and Word. We need to recognize the difference between these two systems and choose God's kingdom! Needless to say, as we immerse ourselves in the Word of God, we will find many things that will need to be changed. These changes have always been a part of the sanctification process of those that walk with God.

The Feasts of the LORD Study Guide | DVD

The Apostle Paul does a wonderful job of showing how believers come into the faith just as Abraham did:

> **Galatians 3:6-9 (NKJV)**
> ⁶just as Abraham *"believed God, and it was accounted to him for righteousness."* ⁷Therefore know that *only* those who are of faith are sons of Abraham. ⁸And the Scripture, foreseeing that God would justify the Gentiles by faith, preached the gospel to Abraham beforehand, *saying, "In you all the nations shall be blessed."* ⁹So then those who *are* of faith are blessed with believing Abraham.

Before God called Abram, he was a pagan, a gentile (one without covenant with God) and a citizen of Babylon. When Abram believed God, he left everything of Babylon behind and "crossed over" into a new way of living. He became a "Hebrew." Listen to what God promises him:

> **Genesis 17:1 (NKJV)**
> ¹When Abram was ninety-nine years old, the Lord appeared to Abram and said to him, "I *am* Almighty God; walk before Me and be blameless.

To our English ears, this either sounds like a challenge or even an ultimatum, but it is not! It is a very powerful promise. In the Hebrew, God declares who He is and then gives this promise in only three words. Let's look at them.

> **Walk**: Strongs # H1980 הָלַךְ halak {haw-lak'} [1]
> **Meaning:** 1) to go, walk, come 1a) (Qal) 1a1) to go, walk, come, depart, proceed, move, go away 1a2) to die, live, manner of life

---

[1] Strong's Enhanced Lexicon. BibleWorks for Windows 7.0. BibleWorks, LLC, Norfolk, VA. Copyright © 2006.

Biblical Life Publishing

(fig.) 1b) (Piel) 1b1) to walk 1b2) to walk (fig.) 1c) (Hithpael) 1c1) to traverse 1c2) to walk about 1d) (Niphal) to lead, bring, lead away, carry, cause to walk
Origin: akin to 03212, a primitive root; TWOT - 498; v
Usage: AV - go 217, walk 156, come 16, ...away 7, ...along 6, misc 98; 500

Before Me: Strongs # H6440 פָּנִים paniym {paw-neem'} pl. (but always as sing.) of an unused noun hn<P' paneh {paw-neh'} [2]

Meaning: 1) face 1a) face, faces 1b) presence, person 1c) face (of seraphim or cherubim) 1d) face (of animals) 1e) face, surface (of ground) 1f) as adv of loc/temp 1f1) before and behind, toward, in front of, forward, formerly, from beforetime, before 1g) with prep 1g1) in front of, before, to the front of, in the presence of, in the face of, at the face or front of, from the presence of, from before, from before the face of
Origin: from 06437; TWOT - 1782a; n m
Usage: AV - before 1137, face 390, presence 76, because 67, sight 40, countenance 30, from 27, person 21, upon 20, of 20, ...me 18, against 17, ...him 16, open 13, for 13, toward 9, misc 195; 2109

Perfect: Strongs #H8549 תָּמִים tamiym {taw-meem'} [3]

Meaning: 1) complete, whole, entire, sound 1a) complete, whole, entire 1b) whole, sound, healthful 1c) complete, entire (of time) 1d) sound, wholesome, unimpaired, innocent, having integrity 1e) what is complete or entirely in accord with truth and fact (neuter adj/subst)
Origin: from 08552; TWOT - 2522d; adj
Usage: AV - without blemish 44, perfect 18, upright 8, without spot 6, uprightly 4, whole 4, sincerely 2, complete 1, full 1, misc 3; 91

I believe God was giving Abram this powerful promise: "Abram, I AM Almighty God. Come and walk in My presence and you will become complete, whole, sound, healthful, innocent, and a

---

[2] Ibid
[3] Ibid

person of integrity that walks in truth." **_This is the call for every Hebrew!_**

Jesus made a similar call:

> **Matthew 4:19 (NKJV)**
> [19] Then He said to them, "**_Follow Me, and I will make you_** fishers of men."

Jesus calls to all men just like He did to Abram. "Come, walk in My presence and I will make you whole!"

Just like Abram, part of the process of "walking" and "making" is to "crossover" from the ways of Babylon to the ways of God. This is the call, challenge and promise for every believer!

In the Beginning and the Cycles of the Kingdom

As Different as Night and Day

As we "crossover" from the system of Babylon to the ways of God, we need to examine the Word of God to see how God says things are supposed to be. God's Kingdom will always come in line with the way God has revealed things, not necessarily the way everyone else does them! We will find that when we compare the two, they are as different as "night and day." In fact, the first thing that we are going to look at is: "when does a new day start biblically?"

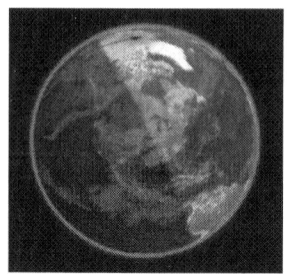

Genesis 1:5 (NKJV)
⁵ God called the light Day, and the darkness He called Night. <u>So the evening and the morning were the first day</u>.

When God created the heavens and the earth, the first day started in darkness and moved toward the light. When we enter back into the way that God made things, the new day starts at sunset and not sunrise!

Law of First Mention

Many do not realize that there is a science to studying and interpreting the Word of God. This science is called "hermeneutics." Within this science of biblical interpretation, there are many hermeneutical laws (or principles) that must be followed to properly understand and rightly divide the Word of God. One of those principles is the "Law of First Mention." Let's look at a basic definition of this law:

> *The Meaning of the Law of First Mention* [4]
>
> *The law of first mention may be said to be the principle that requires one to go to that portion of the Scriptures where a doctrine is mentioned for the first time and to study the first occurrence of the same in order to get the fundamental inherent meaning of that doctrine. When we thus see the first appearance, which is usually in the simplest form, we can then examine the doctrine in other*

---

[4] Taken from the website of the Biblical Research Society.
http://www.biblicalresearch.info/page56.html

portions of the Word that were given later. We shall see that the fundamental concept in the first occurrence remains dominant as a rule, and colors all later additions to that doctrine. In view of this fact, it becomes imperative that we understand the law of first mention.

Whenever we see God giving a definition in the Word of God (and especially the Torah), we will find that definition used all the way from Genesis to Revelation. Lack of knowledge of this one law has caused many to err in their interpretation of the Word of God.

So, biblically, a new day always starts at sunset and not sunrise.

The Prophetic Significance of When a New Day Starts

This planet started in darkness until God acted. Only with the intervention of the Almighty did light come into the world. What does this teach us?

> 1. Man would, like the world, end up in darkness. He would require intervention from the Creator to move him into the light. God calls light "good" because it is His opinion of His plan of Salvation - it was for the good of mankind!
>
> 2. When God begins to "speak" to man (as He did with His creation), man must respond to His "speaking" by moving away from darkness and into the full light of God. This is the process of sanctification - moving from the ways of darkness into the ways of God's light.

God's Weekly Cycle

> **Genesis 2:1-3 (NKJV)**
> [1] Thus the heavens and the earth, and all the host of them, were finished. [2] And on the seventh day God ended His work which He had done, and He rested on the seventh day from all His work which He had done. [3] Then God blessed the seventh day and sanctified it, because in it He rested from all His work which God had created and made.

Why are there only seven days in a week? We have seven days because God made it that way! Man has tried several times to deviate from God's established week. Both the French Republic and the Soviet Union tried to establish a ten day week with dismal outcomes.

The law of first mention holds true with the Sabbath - it has always been and will always be on the seventh day. Only manmade tradition has changed the Sabbath from the seventh day to the first. Jesus told us why God made the Sabbath:

> **Mark 2:27 (NKJV)**
> [27] And He said to them, "***The Sabbath was made for man***, and not man for the Sabbath."

We will study the concept of the Sabbath in great detail in the upcoming study "The Sabbath: A Biblical Investigation."

Biblical Months

Biblical months go from New Moon to New Moon rather than by solar cycles. The New Moon is known in scripture as *Rosh-Hodesh* (head of the month). Let's look at the moon cycle:

The Feasts of the LORD Study Guide | DVD

Facts about Establishing When a New Month Starts

1.   There are several days in which the New Moon can be established. It also requires two witnesses that physically see the New Moon and provide testimony to leadership. This can be complicated with a cloudy or overcast sky. The biblical term "no man knows the day or hour" refers both to the sighting of the New Moon and the Feast of Trumpets (which begins on the New Moon).

2.   Upon the establishment of the nation of Israel, the two witnesses would present themselves at the gates of Jerusalem. They would be told to "come up hither" to present their witness to the High Priest to establish the New Moon.

3.   The New Moon shows prophetically several things about mankind:

(1) All start in darkness.
(2) The only light man can achieve is the reflection of the light of God.
(3) Man also has a propensity to wander away from God and to go back into darkness.
(4) God is always a God of new beginnings!

God's Seasonal Cycles

Genesis 8:22 (NKJV)
22 "While the earth remains, Seedtime and harvest, Cold and heat, Winter and summer, And day and night Shall not cease."

The seasonal cycles were established by God and remain as a testimony about the Creator.

Other Cycles

Although it is not in the scope of this teaching, there are many other cycles we can mention.

1. Women have a monthly cycle of life.
2. We all have spiritual cycles. (See my teaching on "The Seasonal Life of the Believer.")
3. We also have cycles within our emotions/soul and our physical bodies. (Bio-rhythms.)

The Feasts of the LORD Study Guide | DVD

Our Spinning Galaxy

This is a picture of our galaxy - the Milky Way.[5] To emphasize that God's Kingdom has a cycle to it, God has placed us within a spiral galaxy!

To miss the significance that God places on His established cycles is to miss the ebbs and flows of the Kingdom of God. When we miss God's cycles, we end up like the children of Israel in the wilderness; we wander around in pointless circles. When we enter into God's cycles through the guiding of the Holy Spirit, we enter into cycles of blessing, enrichment and growth.

---

[5] Graphic taken from the website: Atlas of the Universe. (www.atlasoftheuniverse.com)

The Feasts of the LORD Study Guide | DVD

The Cycles of God's Feasts

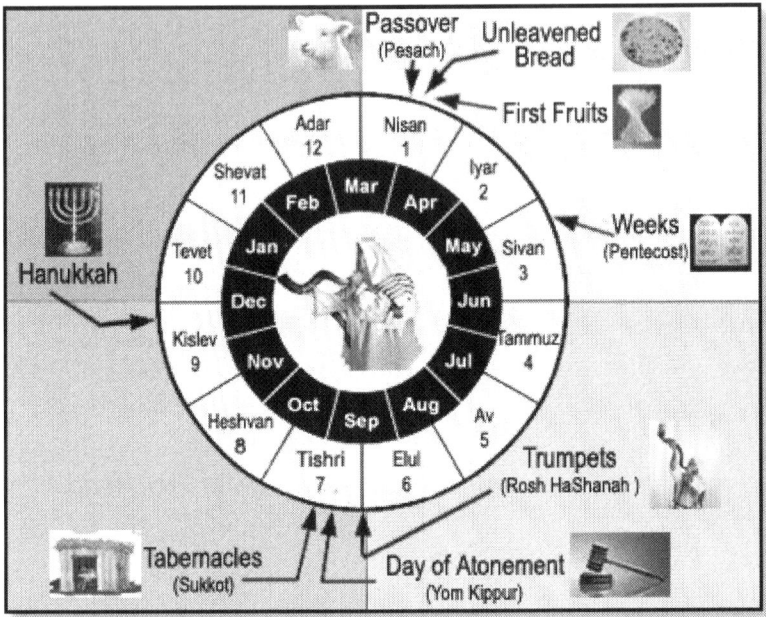

Leviticus 23:1-2 (NKJV)
¹ And the Lord spoke to Moses, saying, ² "Speak to the children of Israel, and say to them: 'The _**feasts of the Lord**_, which you shall proclaim *to be* holy convocations, _**these are My feasts**_.

The first thing that we need to notice in this scripture is that God does NOT call these Feasts the "Feasts of the Jews." The Feasts He introduces to the nation of Israel are His FEASTS. All those that become a part of the nation of Israel may participate in these Feasts.

The Feasts of the LORD Study Guide | DVD

What are We a Part of?

Ephesians 2:11-14 (NKJV)

¹¹ Therefore remember that you, once Gentiles in the flesh--who are called Uncircumcision by what is called the Circumcision made in the flesh by hands-- ¹² that at that time you were <u>without Christ, being aliens from the commonwealth of Israel and strangers from the covenants of promise, having no hope and without God in the world.</u> ¹³ But now in Christ Jesus you <u>who once were far off have been brought near</u> by the blood of Christ. ¹⁴ For He Himself is our peace, who has made both one, and has broken down the middle wall of separation,

Romans 11:11-27 (NKJV)

¹¹ I say then, have they stumbled that they should fall? Certainly not! But through their fall, to provoke them to jealousy, <u>salvation *has come* to the Gentiles.</u> ¹² Now if their fall *is* riches for the world, and their failure riches for the Gentiles, how much more their fullness! ¹³ For I speak to you Gentiles; inasmuch as I am an apostle to the Gentiles, I magnify my ministry, ¹⁴ if by any means I may provoke to jealousy *those who are* my flesh and save some of them. ¹⁵ For if their being cast away *is* the reconciling of the world, what *will* their acceptance *be* but life from the dead? ¹⁶ For if the firstfruit *is* holy, the lump *is* also *holy;* and if the root *is* holy, so *are* the branches. ¹⁷ And if some of the branches were broken off, and you, being a wild olive tree, <u>were grafted in among them,</u> and <u>with them became a partaker of the root and fatness of the olive tree,</u> ¹⁸ do not boast against the branches. But if you do boast<u>, *remember that* you do not support the root, but the root supports you.</u> ¹⁹ You will say then, "Branches were broken off that I might be grafted in." ²⁰ Well *said.* Because of unbelief they were broken off, and you stand by faith. Do not be haughty, but fear. ²¹ For if

God did not spare the natural branches, He may not spare you either. ²² Therefore consider the goodness and severity of God: on those who fell, severity; but toward you, goodness, if you continue in *His* goodness. Otherwise you also will be cut off. ²³ And they also, <u>if they do not continue in unbelief, will be grafted in, for God is able to graft them in again</u>. ²⁴ For if you were cut out of the olive tree which is wild by nature, and were grafted contrary to nature into a cultivated olive tree, how much more will these, who *are* natural *branches,* be grafted into their own olive tree? ²⁵ For I do not desire, brethren, <u>that you should be ignorant of this mystery</u>, lest you should be wise in your own opinion, ***that blindness in part has happened to Israel until the fullness of the Gentiles has come in.*** ²⁶ ***And so all Israel will be saved***, as it is written: *"The Deliverer will come out of Zion, And He will turn away ungodliness from Jacob;* ²⁷ *For this is My covenant with them, When I take away their sins."*

Through Messiah, we were grafted in as citizens of Israel. When all the Gentiles that are to be grafted into Israel are saved, then the blinders will be taken completely off of Israel and ALL OF ISRAEL will be saved.

Notice that Paul did not say "the Jews were blinded." He said "Israel." There were two types of blindness that were placed on Israel until the end of days:

| Blindness upon the Jewish part of Israel | Blindness to who Messiah is. |
| Blindness upon the new Gentile part of Israel | Blindness to the Torah (Moses). |

Revelation tells us something wonderful will happen when the blindness over Israel is completely lifted:

> **Revelation 15:3-4 (NKJV)**
> ³ They sing the song of Moses, the servant of God, and the song of the Lamb, saying: "Great and marvelous *are* Your works, Lord God Almighty! Just and true *are* Your ways, O King of the saints! ⁴ Who shall not fear You, O Lord, and glorify Your name? For *You* alone *are* holy. For all nations shall come and worship before You, For Your judgments have been manifested."

The blindness is beginning to lift in our day. Scores of Jews are accepting Jesus as the Messiah, and scores of believers are seeing the need for Torah!

What Are the Feasts?

To understand this, we need to look at the Hebrew word translated "feasts" in Leviticus 23:

> **Feasts:** Strongs # H4150 מוֹעֵד mow`ed {mo-ade'} or מֹעֵד mo`ed {mo-ade'} or (fem.) מוֹעָדָה mow`adah (2 Chr 8:13) {mo-aw-daw'} [6]
> **Meaning:** 1) appointed place, appointed time, meeting 1a) appointed time 1a1) appointed time (general) 1a2) sacred season, set feast, appointed season 1b) appointed meeting 1c) appointed place 1d) appointed sign or signal 1e) tent of meeting
> **Origin:** from 03259; TWOT - 878b; n m
> **Usage:** AV - congregation 150, feast 23, season 13, appointed 12, time 12, assembly 4, solemnity 4, solemn 2, days 1, sign 1, synagogues 1; 223

---

[6] Ibid.

These are times appointed by Almighty God for us to meet with Him. These appointments have never been changed in the scripture. Manmade traditions have changed them to take us out of rhythm with the Kingdom of God.

These special appointed times with God are also divine rehearsals. By remembering what God has done in the past, we PREPARE for what He is going to do in the future.

Isaiah 46:9-10 (NKJV)
⁹ Remember the former things of old, For I *am* God, and *there is* no other; *I am* God, and *there is* none like Me, ¹⁰ Declaring the end from the beginning, And from ancient times *things* that are not *yet* done, Saying, 'My counsel shall stand, And I will do all My pleasure,'

Remembering is a very Hebraic concept. When we remember what God has done for us, it builds power within our spirit man. The whole reason we celebrate communion is to remember what Jesus has done for us. Therefore, there is a spiritual strength released in us when we take time for God's appointments to remember.

The questions that we must ask ourselves are:

> "What feasts am I keeping?"
> "What are they really reminding me of?"
> "What are they preparing me for?"

The Feasts of the LORD Study Guide | DVD

"Are they strengthening me for today & tomorrow?"

Review Questions

1. What is the sanctification process in the life of the believer?

2. What do manmade traditions do in our lives?

The Feasts of the LORD Study Guide | DVD

3. How is our walk with God similar to that of Abraham?

4. What is the law of first mention?

5. When the day starts at evening, as given to us in Word of God, what is it telling us?

6. What are biblical months based on and what can we learn from it?

7. Is a believer a part of Israel?

8. What are the Feasts of the LORD?

The Feasts of the LORD Study Guide | DVD

Lesson Two

The Basics for Understanding Babylon

In our last lesson, I introduced you to many concepts from the Word of God that have been forgotten by the Body of Christ. I also shared that there was a kingdom (and its system) that was constantly warring against the Kingdom and principles of God. This warring system is called Babylon. In this lesson, we are going to tear the cloak of secrecy away and let the light of truth shine on the history of Babylon.

The Babylonian Yeast of Paganism

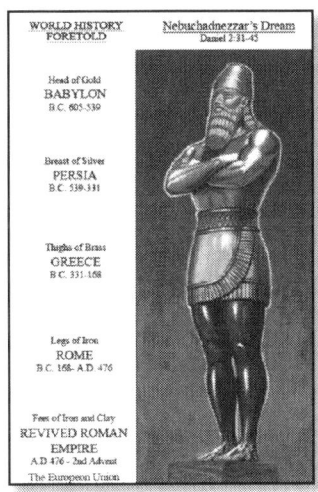

Just like in the dream Nebuchadnezzar had in Daniel 2:31-45, we see the effects of Babylon stream down from the head of gold (Babylon) to the feet of iron and clay (the Revised Roman Empire). These influences were not just about political or military power as most commentators conclude. These influences were like a three-fold cord, which includes: politics, economics, and religion. As we examine the origins of the religious system of Babylon, we will find that it did infect all the cultures represented in Daniel 2.

The Book of Revelation instructs us to:

> **Revelation 18:4-5 (NKJV)**
> [4] And I heard another voice from heaven saying, "Come out of her, my people, lest you share in her sins, and lest you receive of her plagues. [5] For her sins have reached to heaven, and God has remembered her iniquities.

How can we come out of what we do not recognize? In this lesson, we will have an extremely condensed introduction to the origin of all paganism and occult practices in the world today.

The Seed of Babylon was on the Ark

> **Genesis 10:1 (NKJV)**
> [1] Now this *is* the genealogy of the sons of Noah: Shem, Ham, and Japheth. And sons were born to them after the flood.

Ham carried the seeds of evil within his heart. Those seeds soon took root after the flood.

> **Genesis 9:20-24 (NKJV)**
> [20] And Noah began *to be* a farmer, and he planted a vineyard. [21] Then he drank of the wine and was drunk, and became uncovered in his tent. [22] And Ham, the father of Canaan, saw the nakedness of his father, and told his two brothers outside. [23] But Shem and Japheth took a garment, laid *it* on both their shoulders, and went backward and covered the nakedness of their father. Their faces *were* turned away, and they did not see their father's nakedness. [24] So Noah awoke from his wine, and knew what his younger son had done to him.

There are many speculations as to what really occurred in verse 22. Here are some of the possibilities from both Rabbinic and Christian commentators:

> **Theory 1**: Ham showed great dishonor both by seeing Noah's nakedness and then by insultingly telling his brothers.
>
> **Theory 2**: Several Rabbinic sources hypothesize that Ham sexually violated Noah while Canaan watched just outside the tent. This explains the reason why Canaan was cursed in verse 25.
>
> **Theory 3**: In Leviticus, we are told that having sexual relations with the wife of your father is considered "uncovering his nakedness." (Lev 18:8)

No matter how you read through all of this (whether pride, dishonor or sexual perversion), it is the seeds of evil within Ham's heart. The other two brothers took immediate action to keep their father's dignity intact and received a blessing for it.

Following the Seed of Ham

> **Genesis 10:6 (NKJV)**
> ⁶ The sons of Ham *were* Cush, Mizraim, Put, and Canaan.

The four sons of Ham created nations as their offspring multiplied.

To get a better understanding of the people and nations that came from Ham, we will turn to Dake's Annotated Reference Bible:

The Sons of Ham [7]

1. Cush (Gen. 10:6-12; 1Chr. 1:8-10; Isa. 11:11), progenitor of various Ethiopian tribes that settled south of Egypt and also overran Arabia, Babylonia, and India.

2. Mizraim (Gen. 10:6,13-14; 1Chr. 1:8-11), progenitor of various Egyptian tribes. Mizraim means "double." Tribes of the double Egypt (upper and lower Egypt), called the land of Ham, came from him (Ps. 78:51; 105:23-27; 106:22). The Philistines also came from Mizraim (Gen. 10:14).

3. Phut (Gen. 10:6; Ezek. 27:10), progenitor of the Libyans and other tribes in northern Africa (Ezek. 27:10; 30:5; 38:5; Jer. 46:9; Nah. 3:9).

4. Canaan (Gen. 10:6,15-19; 9:18-27; 1Chr. 1:8-13), progenitor of peoples that settled mainly in Palestine, Arabia, Tyre, Sidon, and other parts of the land promised to Abraham. These nations are often mentioned in connection with Israel (Gen. 10:15-19; 15:18-21; Dt. 7:1-3; Josh. 12).

It only takes a quick glance to see that all of these groups forsook the knowledge of God and became pagan. The two most notable are:

Cush: The father of Nimrod and the co-founder of Babylon.
Mizraim: The founder of Egypt.

This is one of the reasons that the religions of Babylon and Egypt are exactly alike - except for the names of their gods. It's all in the family!

---

[7] Finis J. Dake, *Dake's Annotated Reference Bible*, (Lawrenceville: Dake Publishing, Inc., 2007), WORD*search* CROSS e-book, Under: "Chapter 10".

In understanding the foundation and development of all paganism and occultism in the world, you have to understand the three most significant characters in the foundations of Babylon.

Nimrod

Nimrod was the son of Cush and the co-founder of Babylon.

> **Genesis 10:8-10a (NKJV)**
> ⁸ Cush begot Nimrod; he began to be a mighty one on the earth. ⁹ He was a mighty hunter before the Lord; therefore it is said, "Like Nimrod the mighty hunter before the Lord." ¹⁰ And the beginning of his kingdom was Babel . . .

How did Nimrod become a mighty one in the earth? He was a great hunter. Wild animals posed a great problem to the people of his time. His ability to hunt the animals effectively allowed the people to dwell in safety. He then used his service as a platform to build his own personal power. Let's look at what commentator Matthew Henry wrote about Nimrod:

NIMROD THE FIRST MONARCH. (10:8-14)[8]

Nimrod was a great man in his day; he began to be mighty in the earth, Those before him were content to be upon the same level with their neighbours, and though every man bare rule in his own house, yet no man pretended any further. Nimrod was resolved to lord it over his neighbours. The spirit of the giants before the flood, who became mighty men, and men of renown, Gen 6:4, revived in him. **Nimrod was a great hunter**. Hunting then was the method of preventing the hurtful increase of wild beasts. This required great courage and address, and thus gave an opportunity for Nimrod to command others, and gradually attached a number of men to one leader. From such a beginning, it is likely, that Nimrod began to rule, and to force others to submit. He invaded his neighbours' rights and properties, and persecuted innocent men; endeavouring to make all his own by force and violence. He carried on his oppressions and violence in defiance of God himself. **Nimrod was a great ruler**. Some way or other, by arts or arms, he got into power, and so founded a monarchy, which was the terror of the mighty, and bid fair to rule all the world. **Nimrod was a great builder**. Observe in Nimrod the nature of ambition. It is boundless; much would have more, and still cries, Give, give. It is restless; Nimrod, when he had four cities under his command, could not be content till he had four more. It is expensive; Nimrod will rather be at the charge of rearing cities, than not have the honour of ruling them. It is daring, and will stick at nothing. Nimrod's name signifies rebellion; tyrants to men are rebels to God. The days are coming, when conquerors will no longer be spoken of with praise, as in man's partial

---

[8] Matthew Henry, *Matthew Henry Concise Bible Commentary*, WORD*search* CROSS e-book, Under: "Chapter 10".

The Feasts of the LORD Study Guide | DVD

histories, but be branded with infamy, as in the impartial records of the Bible.

There are several ways to look at the name "Nimrod." First, let's look at the basic Strongs and Brown-Drivers-Biggs definition:

Nimrod: **Strongs # H5248** נִמְרוֹד Nimrowd {nim-rode'} or

נִמְרֹד Nimrod {nim-rode'}

Meaning: Nimrod = "rebellion" or "the valiant" 1) the son of Cush, grandson of Ham, and great grandson of Noah; a mighty hunter, he established an empire in the area of Babylon and Assyria
Origin: probably of foreign origin;; n pr m
Usage: AV - Nimrod 4; 4

The second way to look at the name of Nimrod would be to look at it like a Rabbi would. Rabbi Daniel Lapin, in his series entitled "Tower of Power: Decoding the Secrets of Babel" provides this simple, yet effective, way of understanding the Hebrew:

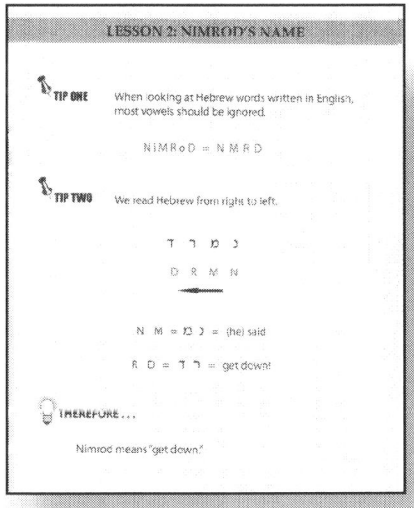

Biblical Life Publishing

The Feasts of the LORD Study Guide | DVD

Nimrod developed his political, military and religious power by exalting himself above the people. The people were brought under Nimrod to have safety, some willingly and others by coercion.

Nimrod was known for:

- Developing a new religion that sprang from his cities. This religion warred against the knowledge of God in the earth.
- Developing the first walled cities for protection.
- Developing an economic system within his cities so that men would rely on each other rather than God.

Another Thing Nimrod is Known For

"Cupid is depicted with a bow and arrow, a reminder of Nimrod being a "mighty hunter"

How did Cupid originate with Nimrod. It is said that even as a child, he possessed the power to cause his own mother to be sexually attracted to him.

Maybe the answer to "Noah's nakedness" is answered in Nimrod?

As Nimrod grew up, he married his own mother, who became Queen of Babylon. Her name was "Semiramis."

Under Nimrod, child sacrifice was one of the abominations he established as worship to a demon god named Molech. Molech was the god of pleasure and prosperity.

Baby offered to Molech.

Later as the power and reputation of Babylon grew, righteous Seth confronted Nimrod and killed him for the abominations he had established in Babylon. Jewish tradition tells us that Seth cut Nimrod's body into pieces and sent them to the cities Nimrod had established with the warning: "If you continue these practices, this will happen to you too." Therefore, many took these practices underground and they became hidden (or occult).

At the death of Nimrod, Semiramis had to keep her abominations going in Babylon. She established a religion around Nimrod ascending to become the sun-god. Thus, sun-worship was established.

The Feasts of the LORD Study Guide | DVD

Semiramis

Semiramis was the mother/wife of Nimrod and continued the building of Babylon and its influence after his death. She was now the mother of god. She ruled Babylon with an iron fist. The rabbis note several other things about her:

- Her beauty was so astounding that she stopped a battle by just walking through the battlefield.

- She invented crucifixion to stop those that opposed her power. This may have been in response to Seth killing Nimrod for his crimes against God and man.

Several years after the death of Nimrod, Semiramis became pregnant. She claimed her pregnancy was by a divine act in which the rays from the sun-god impregnated her. This time was marked as a divine date occurring on the Vernal Equinox. We know this date as Easter. The timing of Easter was later changed by the Catholic Church. The First Council of Nicaea (325 A.D.) established the date of Easter as the first Sunday after the full moon (the Paschal Full Moon) following the Vernal Equinox.

She gave birth to Tammuz on the Winter Solstice. Originally the Winter Solstice fell on December 25 until the Gregorian calendar

(1582 A.D.) was instituted. With the new calendar, which we use today, the Winter Solstice falls on December 21.

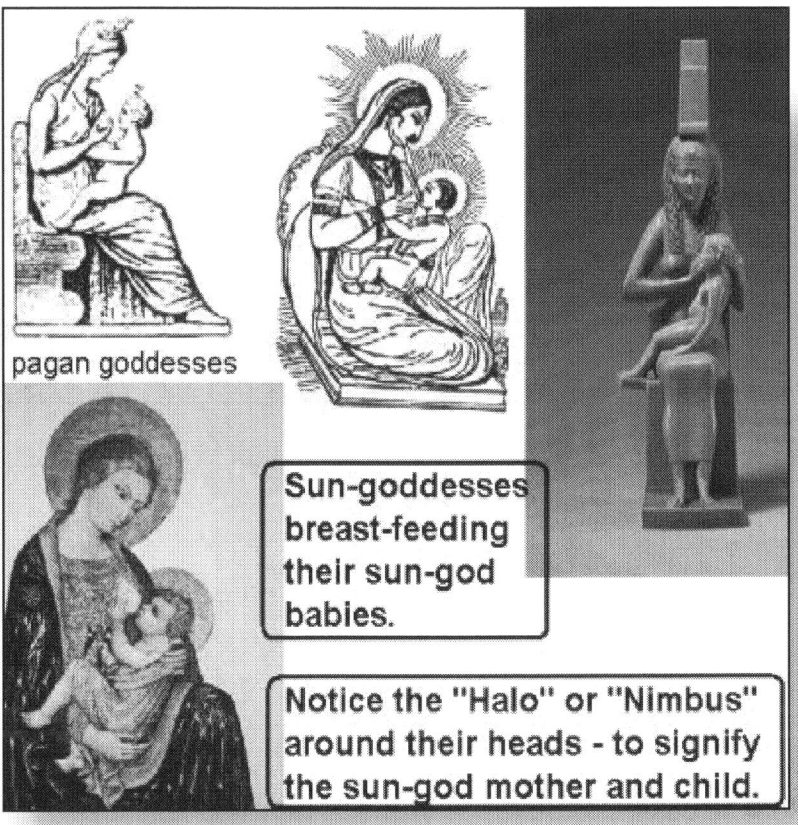

Semiramis told the people of Babylon that Nimrod had come back through what became reincarnation. The womb that gave them Nimrod had produced him in another form: Tammuz. The new Babylonian god was born and, of course, she was the mother of god twice over. The Queen of Heaven with her child-god became a powerful symbol in Babylon and is present to this day in various forms throughout paganism.

The Feasts of the LORD Study Guide | DVD

Notice the halo or nimbus around the heads in these illustrations. This did not represent holiness, it represented the sun.

After the death of Semiramis, she was exalted to permanent godhood as well as the Queen of Heaven. She would descend back to earth to commemorate the conception of Tammuz in a multicolored egg. Worshippers would get up for sun-rise services to see if they could witness her descending; those that saw her were blessed for the next year. To prove her divinity, she would give a rabbit the power to lay eggs – which was one of her many symbols.

Other Practices of Easter

During the time of her conceiving Tammuz, the priests in their temples would impregnate young women. These women would then give birth around December 25 to honor the birth of Tammuz. These same children would be sacrificed in honor of the spring goddess and their blood was used to color the "Easter eggs." To this day, Greek Orthodox still insists that Easter eggs can only be dyed blood red.

The Feasts of the LORD Study Guide | DVD

Tammuz

Tammuz ruled beside his mother until he was forty. During his fortieth year, he was killed by a wild boar while hunting. It became a practice to weep and fast for forty days prior to his time of conception each year. We find women weeping for Tammuz in the Temple of God – an abomination!

Ezekiel 8:13-14 (NKJV)
13 And He said to me, "Turn again, *and* you will see greater abominations that they are doing."
14 So He brought me to the door of the north gate of the Lord's house; and to my dismay, women were sitting there weeping for Tammuz.

It wouldn't be Easter without it.

Another pagan practice that occurred after the 40 days of weeping and fasting was to kill what killed their god and feast upon it.

The 40 days of weeping and fasting became known as "Lent." It has been a tradition for thousands of years to eat roast pork (or ham) during Easter.

Tammuz is known by many other names. One of them was Mithra. The Mithra religion was very popular among the Roman soldiers and Constantine used it to his advantage. The Roman Universal (Catholic) Church was born.

More Information on the Mystery Religions

Over the years, I have read dozens of books, articles and countless websites to compile this condensed explanation. If you would like to further your own personal research, here are several places to start:

"The Two Babylons" by Alexander Hislop.
"Babylon Mystery Religion: Ancient and Modern" by Ralph Woodrow.
"Fossilized Customs: The Pagan Sources of Popular Customs" by Lew White.

The Feasts of the LORD Study Guide | DVD

Review Questions

1. What cultures or systems has Babylon influenced over the last several millennia?

2. Who were the founders of Babylon and Egypt?

3. What does this statement mean: "Nimrod was a mighty hunter before the Lord?"

4. There are two basic definitions of what Nimrod's name means. What are they?

5. What practice did Nimrod institute that resulted in his death?

6. What did Semiramis tell the people after the death of Nimrod?

The Feasts of the LORD Study Guide | DVD

7. How did Semiramis invent reincarnation?

8. What practice was instituted after the death of Semiramis?

9. Describe what "weeping for Tammuz" was and how it is observed today.

Lesson Three

The Feasts of the LORD and Prophecy

I. Different Levels of Understanding Scripture

As we approach various understandings and applications of the Feasts of the LORD, we need to comprehend that there are several levels of interpreting the Word of God. The rabbis understood four levels of interpretation that were used in Torah (and later expanded their use to all of the TaNaKh or Old Testament). The rabbis have always used and looked for acrostics and acronyms (in fact, one was found above Jesus' head on the Cross). TaNaKh stands for Torah, Navi'im, and Ketuvim. In this fashion, when an individual can properly interpret and apply the Word of God, he walks in PaRDeS (Paradise).

> **Deuteronomy 11:21 (KJV)**
> [21] That your days may be multiplied, and the days of your children, in the land which the Lord sware unto your fathers to give them, as the days of heaven upon the earth.

The Feasts of the LORD Study Guide | DVD

P a R D e S

The **Pardes** typology describes four different approaches to Biblical exegesis in rabbinic Judaism (or - simpler - interpretation of text in Torah study). The term, sometimes also spelled **PaRDeS**, is an acronym formed from the name initials of these four approaches, which are:

- **Pe**shat (פְּשָׁט) — "plain" ("simple") or the direct meaning[1].
- **Re**mez (רֶמֶז) — "hints" or the deep (allegoric) meaning beyond just the literal sense.
- **De**rash (דְּרַשׁ) — from Hebrew *darash*: "inquire" ("seek") — the comparative (midrashic) meaning, as given through similar occurrences.
- **S**od (סוֹד) (pronounced with a long O as in gold) — "secret" ("mystery") or the mystical meaning, as given through inspiration or revelation.

Each type of *Pardes* interpretation examines the extended meaning of a text. As a general rule, the extended meaning never contradicts the base meaning. The *Peshat* means the plain or contextual meaning of the text. *Remez* is the allegorical meaning. *Derash* includes the metaphorical meaning, and *Sod* represents the hidden meaning. There is often considerable overlap, for example when legal understandings of a verse are influenced by mystical interpretations or when a "hint" is determined by comparing a word with other instances of the same word. [9]

As we proceed with this study, we will look both at the prophetic significance of the Feasts and at some of the spiritual implications in the life of all believers.

---

[9] Wikipedia Definition. http://en.wikipedia.org/wiki/Pardes_(Jewish_exegesis)

The Feasts of the LORD Study Guide | DVD

Before we go on, would you like to see the acrostic that appeared over the head of Jesus on the Cross? Remember, Jesus said:

> **John 8:28 (KJV)**
> [28] Then said Jesus unto them, When ye have lifted up the Son of man, then shall ye know that I am *he*, and *that* I do nothing of myself; but as my Father hath taught me, I speak these things.

Notice after "I am" that "he" is italicized. This means it was not in the original Greek. The translators did not understand what Jesus was saying, so they added a "he" in the sentence. Jesus was saying "When I am lifted up on the Cross, you will see that I AM." "I AM" is another way of saying the most holy name of God: Yod-Hey-Vav-Hey.

What did Pilate write over the head of Jesus that made the rabbis want to change it?

> **John 19:19-22 (KJV)**
> [19] And Pilate wrote a title, and put *it* on the cross. And the writing was, JESUS OF NAZARETH THE KING OF THE JEWS. [20] This title then read many of the Jews: for the place where Jesus was crucified was nigh to the city: and it was written in Hebrew, *and* Greek, *and* Latin. [21] Then said the chief priests of the Jews to Pilate, Write not, The King of the Jews; but that he said, I am King of the Jews. [22] Pilate answered, What I have written I have written.

The Feasts of the LORD Study Guide | DVD

II. An Overview of the Feasts & Rehearsals

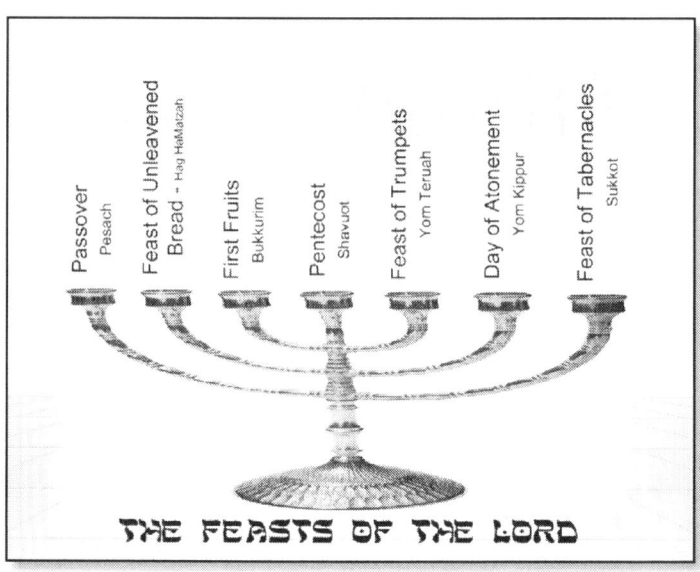

The Feasts of the LORD Study Guide | DVD

Leviticus 23:4 (NKJV)
4 'These *are* the feasts of the Lord, holy convocations which you shall proclaim at their appointed times.

In Leviticus 23, God lists seven times a year that are holy convocations or appointed times to meet with Him. They are:

- Passover - Pesach
- Unleavened Bread - Hag HaMatzah
- First Fruits - Bikkurim
- Pentecost - Shavout
- Trumpets - Yom Teruah
- Day of Atonement - Yom Kippur
- Tabernacles - Sukkot

To get a better understanding of what these holy convocations (or appointed times) mean, I would like to share some insights from an article on the Feasts by Messianic Rabbi Ariel ben-Lyman HaNaviy:

> In both Biblical and Modern Hebrew, the word for "appointed time" is "mo'eyd".
> Interestingly, this meaning conveys the sense of the "dress rehearsals" that occur
> before an actual play. In this way, HaShem masterfully designed the mikra'ey kodesh to act as dress rehearsals for his children. "Of what?" you might ask. **The Feasts of ADONAI are dress rehearsals of Messianic Redemption.** [10]

---

[10] ben-Lyman HaNaviy, Ariel. Mikra'ey Kosesh: Holy Convocations. Article posted in PDF.
http://www.graftedin.com/images/Parashot/00ChaggimOverviewList.pdf

This one statement makes looking into the Feasts paramount for the believer. The Feasts are dress rehearsals of Messianic Redemption - past, present and future. God has been holding rehearsals all these years to prepare us for what Jesus wants to do in our lives and in the future, and we have never shown up! What is the purpose of rehearsals? They are to prepare us for when God begins to move.

I need to point out that this insight about the rehearsals came to the Jewish community **after** the first time that Messiah came. Since the Jewish people were just going through the motions of remembering what God had done in the past, they were not prepared for what Jesus did when He came. Will we repeat their mistake? Without an understanding of the Feasts (what they teach us and do in us), we may find ourselves ill-prepared for the Lord's return!

III. Breaking the Feasts Down

There are seven Feasts. In scripture, the number seven stands for God's plan of redemption, completeness, spiritual matters and perfection. God's redemptive plan is complete and perfect. There is nothing that we can add to it. We can only recognize it and then choose to enter into it.

These seven feasts are then grouped into three seasons: Spring Feasts, Sumer Feast, and Fall Feasts. Each represents a working of Messiah in the life of the believer.

Revelation 1:12-13 (CJB)
^{12} I turned around to see who was speaking to me; and when I had turned, I saw seven gold *menorahs*; ^{13} and among the *menorah*s

was someone like a Son of Man, wearing a robe down to his feet and a gold band around his chest.

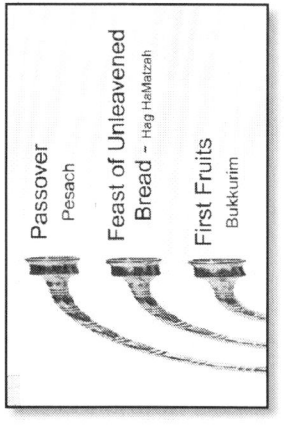

Spring Feasts

The Spring Feasts represent the first time that Jesus came as Messiah ben Joseph - the Suffering Servant. In His first coming, He:

- Became our Passover Lamb: through His shed blood, we have salvation, redemption, deliverance, and freedom.
- Was the unleavened bread that came from Heaven. He was sinless and perfect. He is our example of true biblical sanctification.
- Was the First Fruits offering. He is the firstborn of "many brethren." (Romans 8:29)

Summer Feast

This is where we are now in the redemptive plan of God. The first Shavuot, God gave His commandments on Mount Sinai. On the Shavuot after the resurrection of Jesus, the power of God (the fire from Mount Sinai) was loosed into the hearts of believers to live His commandments and to become witnesses of His work in the earth.

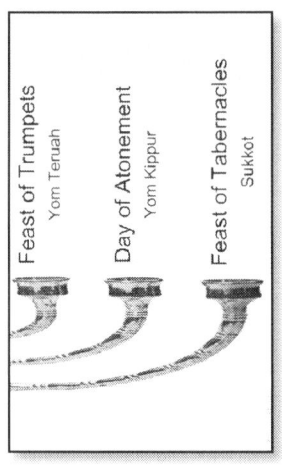

Fall Feasts

To properly understand the Book of Revelation (a Jewish Book), one must lay the Fall Feasts as a template. Without God's template for the second time that Jesus comes (as Messiah ben David), we can wander aimlessly with speculation to its interpretation. Without the appreciation of the Jewishness of the book and its connection to the Hebraic prophets of the Old Testament, we can end up with hundreds of interpretations!

- The Feasts of Trumpets - The catching away of the people of God.
- The Ten Days of Awe (Between Trumpets & Atonement) - Last chance for mankind to repent and to prepare for the King.
- The Day of Atonement - The Day of the LORD and Valley of Armageddon. Jesus comes back as the conquering King.
- Tabernacles - God comes to live among us.

IV. When Seven Becomes Eight

There is a weekly feast also listed in Leviticus 23; it the Sabbath. The Sabbath is a rehearsal of the Millennial Reign of Messiah. Jews and Gentiles, that have partaken of His completed work as Messiah ben Joseph, will be able to enter into His rest.

God has given us the privilege of celebrating Jesus in the Sabbath each week. As we do, we are both preparing for the Millennial Reign of Jesus when He returns, and we get to experience a small portion of that peace now for 24 hours each week!

In this traditional Sabbath setting, we see:

Two Candles: Representing both Jew and Gentile.
Cup of Wine: Representing the blood of Messiah.
Bread: Representing the broken body of Messiah. The bread can also represent the Body of Christ that is being built with living stones.

IV. The Purpose of Every Male Appearing Before the LORD

Deuteronomy 16:16-17 (NKJV)
¹⁶ Three times a year all your males shall appear before the Lord your God in the place which He chooses: at the Feast of Unleavened Bread, at the Feast of Weeks, and at the Feast of Tabernacles; and they shall not appear before the Lord empty-handed. ¹⁷ Every man *shall give* as he is able, according to the blessing of the Lord your God which He has given you.

Not only does God have appointed times that are rehearsals, but three of those times, all men are required to appear before Him and honor the LORD with a gift. There are several things that I need to point out in this scripture:

1. **In the place where He chooses**: I believe this is the place where you are spiritually fed. In the times of Jesus (and David for that matter), men would come to Jerusalem to give their gift. The Word tell us that the "Torah is to come out of Zion." (Isa 2:3) When Jesus comes back to rule and reign for a thousand years, this scripture will be completely fulfilled. In fact, the Word tells us that any nation that does not come to the Feast of Tabernacles, to honor the Messiah, will have no rain in their land the next year. (Zech 14:16,17)

As believers, our primary source of Torah (God's loving instruction) should come from our local congregation. Therefore, the gift should be at your local congregation. If you are not attending a local church, then you give to your primary source of teaching and instruction in God.

2. **Every male shall appear before the LORD**: God always looks to male headship to establish things. In biblical times, the male established the direction of his whole household. This is one of the reasons that Paul and Silas told the Jailor:

> **Acts 16:31 (NKJV)**
> [31] So they said, "Believe on the Lord Jesus Christ, and you will be saved, you and your household."

Satan is trying with all his might to keep men from appearing before the LORD - whether at the Feasts or at Church in general. <u>As we rediscover the Feasts of the LORD, there will be a reactivating of the men with God</u>. We will see revival and empowerment among the men again!

Let's look at the three times that God requires men to appear before Him to see what they are supposed to receive from Him.

Spring Feasts	Summer Feast	Fall Feasts
Messiah ben Joseph - Jesus comes to redeem man.	Jesus baptizes His Church in the Holy Spirit and Fire.	Messiah ben David - Jesus comes as the conquering King.
Man received salvation, the new birth.	Man received power to live for God and be His witness. (A Refiner's Fire)	Man receives the strength to finish the race and make it to the end. (A Finisher's Fire)

The Feasts of the LORD Study Guide | DVD

Review Questions

1. What does PaRDeS stand for?

2. In acrostic, what appeared over the head of Jesus when He was hanging on the Cross?

3. What are the seven Feasts of the LORD?

The Feasts of the LORD Study Guide | DVD

4. What does the term "appointed times" (moed) mean?

5. What do the Spring Feasts represent?

6. What does the Summer Feast represent?

Biblical Life Publishing

7. What do the Fall Feasts represent?

8. What is the significance of every man appearing before the LORD three times a year?

The Feasts of the LORD Study Guide | DVD

Lesson Four

The Spring Feasts - Part 1

As we approach the Spring Feasts, our focus will be on two areas:

1.   What can I learn from the Spring Feasts that is applicable to me as a believer?

2.   How can I observe them without taking anything away from what Jesus has accomplished? (We will cover this aspect in more detail later on in this lesson.)

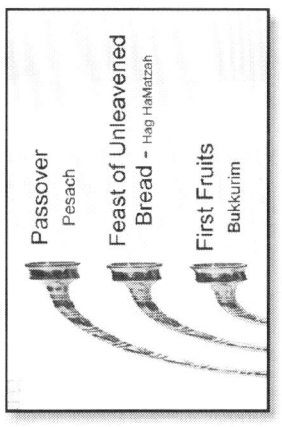

I.   What Comprises the Spring Feasts?

The Spring Feasts are comprised of three biblical feasts:

- Passover
- Unleavened Bread
- First Fruits

Many times all three Feasts are referred to as "Passover" or "Passover Season" by the Jewish community.

Biblical Life Publishing

II. The Scriptures Fulfilled During Passover Week[11]

Prophetic Scripture	Subject	Fulfilled
Zech 9:9	Triumphal Entry	Mark 11:7,9
Psa 8:2	Adored by small children	Matt 21:15
Isa 53:1	Not believed	John 12:37
Psa 41:9	Betrayed by a close friend	Luke 22:47
Zech 11:12	Betrayed for 30 pieces of silver	Matt 26:14,15
Psa 35:11	Accused by false witnesses	Mark 14:57,58
Isa 53:7	Silent to accusations	Mark 15:4,5
Isa 50:6	Spat on and struck	Matt 26:67
Psa 35:19	Hated without reason	John 15:24,25
Isa 53:5	Vicarious sacrifice	Rom 5:6,8
Isa 53:12	Crucified with malefactors	Mark 15:27,28
Zech 12:10	Pierced through hands & feet	John 20:27
Psa 22:7,8	Sneered & mocked	Luke 23:35
Psa 69:9	Was reproached	Rom 15:3
Psa 109:4	Prayed for His enemies	Luke 23:34
Psa 22.17,18	Soldiers gambled for His clothing	Mark 27:34,36
Psa 22:1	Forsaken by God	Matt 27:46
Psa 34:20	No bones broken	John 19:32,33,36
Zech 12:10	His side pierced	John 19:34
Isa 53:9	Buried with the rich	Matt 27:57-60

---

[11] Prophesies of the Messiah. The Open Bible Study Edition. Thomas Nelson Publishers, Nashville, TN. Copyright 1990. Pages 1552-1554.

| Psa 16:10, Psa 49:15 | To be resurrected | Mark 16:6,7 |
| Psa 68:18 | His ascension to God's right hand | Mark 16:19, 1 Cor 15:4, Eph 4:8 |

Twenty-two prophetic promises fulfilled!

III. Background of the Passover

Leviticus 23:5 (NKJV)
[5] On the fourteenth *day* of the first month at twilight *is* the Lord's Passover.

While the children of Israel were in bondage in Egypt, God demanded that His people be set free. On the night that the final plague was to come upon the land, God had His people sacrifice a lamb and place its blood over the doorposts of their homes. When Death saw the blood, it would not enter into that home to take the firstborn that dwelt there.

The Passover observance was a dinner that lasted an hour or two, right before sunset at the beginning of Unleavened Bread. It was a time to remember God's great deliverance of His people from Egypt. It was also a divine rehearsal of the Lamb of God and His sacrifice to free all people from the Pharaoh of this world.

The Feasts of the LORD Study Guide | DVD

IV. Events Around Passover Week

The next two charts were taken from *"Biblical Feasts: A Family Guide to the Biblical Feasts"* by Robin Sampson & Linda Pierce. This is a must have for your library. You can purchase the book from their website at: http://heartofwisdom.com/biblicalholidays/.

	Day	6:00pm-6:00am	Events of Jesus	Matt	Mark	Luke	John
6th Day Before Passover	Nisan 9	Thursday/Friday	Approaches Jerusalem from Jericho. Spends Thursday night at Zacchaeus's home. Sends two disciples ahead for animals. Entry in Bethpage. Cleanses the Temple.	21:1-17		19:1-28	12:1
Weekly Sabbath Before Passover	Nisan 10	Friday/Saturday	Sabbath at Bethany. First of three suppers, two anointings.				12:2-11
4th Day Before Passover	Nisan 11	Saturday/Sunday	Triumphal entrance into Jerusalem. Weeps over city. Enters Temple. Returns to Bethany.	1:8-10 11:1-7,11		9:29-35 19:36-40, 41, 44	12:1 2-19
3rd Day Before Passover	Nisan 12	Sunday/Monday	Returns to Jerusalem. Curses fig tree. At Temple for further cleansing & teaching	21:18, 22	11:12-19	19:45-48	12:20-50
2nd Day Before Passover	Nisan 13	Monday/Tuesday	Returns to Jerusalem. Parables & questions. First great prophecy in the Temple. Second great prophecy on Mt of Olives. Returns to Bethany. Second supper with Simon. Second anointing.	21:23-28 23:39 24:1-51 25:1-46	11:20-33 12:1-44 13:1-37 14:1-9	20:1-9 21:38	
Passover Day of Crucifixion	Nisan 14	Tuesday/Wednesday	Preparation of last supper. Passover supper. Gethsemane, led away to be crucified. Crucified at 9:00am, died at 3:00pm, buried at 6:00pm	26 27	14 15	22 23	13 19

Biblical Life Publishing

Sabbath of Unleavened Bread	Nisan 15	Wednesday/ Thursday	First night, first day in the tomb.				
2nd Day of Unleavened Bread	Nisan 16	Thursday/ Friday	Second night, second day in the tomb.				
Weekly Sabbath First Fruits	Nisan 17	Friday/ Saturday	Third night, third day in the tomb. Arose at the end of the Sabbath at sunset.	28:1-10	16:1-18	24:1-49	20:1-23

V. Passover Observance & Messianic Significance

Passover Observance	Messianic Significance
The lamb was without blemish.	Jesus was examined and found without blemish. (Matt 21:23; 27:1-2; 11-14; 17-26; Luke 3:2; John 11:49-53.
The lamb was a male of the first year.	Jesus was the firstborn Son of God.
The lamb was set aside for four days on the tenth of Nisan.	Jesus entered Jerusalem and the Temple on public display for four days on the tenth of Nisan.
The penalty was imposed the moment the lamb was chosen.	Christ received the death penalty for our sin before He was born.
The lamb was killed between evenings at 3:00pm.	Jesus died in the ninth hour, 3:00pm. (Mark 15:33-37.
The lamb's bones were not broken (Ex 12:46, Num 9:12).	Jesus' bones were not broken. (Ps 34:20; John 19:31)
The blood of the lamb applied to the door saved the Israelites' firstborn.	The blood of Jesus saves us.
The body of the lamb must be eaten the same night (Ex 12:8).	Jesus was crucified, suffered, and died in the same night.
No work was to be done on the Passover. The Israelites could not save themselves. Even if they would have spent all the night in prayer, the destroying angel would have broken in upon them, and slain their first-born, if the blood was not on the door.	The blood of Jesus saves us, not our works. (1 Peter 1:18-21).

VI. Other Significant Things About Passover

    a.   Eat All the Lamb

Exodus 12:8-10 (NKJV)
[8] Then they shall eat the flesh on that night; roasted in fire, with unleavened bread *and* with bitter *herbs* they shall eat it. [9] Do not eat it raw, nor boiled at all with water, but roasted in fire--its head with its legs and its entrails. [10] You shall let none of it remain until morning, and what remains of it until morning you shall burn with fire.

They were instructed to "eat all the lamb." Too many Christians are picky about what they will and will not allow the sacrifice of Jesus to do for them. Some reject healing. Some refuse to deal with iniquity. Others refuse to deal with mental wounds, such as rejection.

Isaiah 53:3-5 (NKJV)
[3] He is despised and rejected by men, A Man of sorrows and acquainted with grief. And we hid, as it were, *our* faces from Him; He was despised, and we did not esteem Him. [4] Surely He has borne our griefs And carried our sorrows; Yet we esteemed Him stricken, Smitten by God, and afflicted. [5] But He *was* wounded for our transgressions, *He was* bruised for our iniquities; The chastisement for our peace *was* upon Him, And by His stripes we are healed.

The Feasts of the LORD Study Guide | DVD

b. The Unleavened Bread

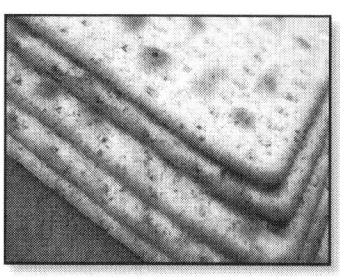

God always uses word pictures, illustrations, etc. to help us understand what He is doing and what He will do for us in the future. Such things are a part of the Hebraic mindset displayed in scripture.

Unleavened bread is:

- Pierced
- Striped
- Bruised
- In its use, it is broken.

Jesus referred to His flesh as "bread." His body was pierced, striped, bruised, and broken for you and I.

c. The Afikomen Bag

Afikoman (Hebrew language: אפיקומן, based on Greek, *epikomen* or *epikomion* [επί Κομός], meaning "that which comes after" or "dessert") is a half-piece of matzo which is broken in the early stages of the Passover Seder and set aside to be eaten as a dessert after the meal.[12]

---

[12] http://en.wikipedia.org/wiki/Afikoman

The Afikomen Bag is used to store the three full sheets of unleavened bread for the Passover. During the Passover Seder, all three pieces are taken out at various times and placed back in. Then the middle piece, representing Isaac, is taken out and broken in half. One piece is wrapped in a white cloth or handkerchief and hidden. The child that finds it receives a reward.

Isaac is a type and shadow of Messiah. "That which comes after" the Passover is the Messiah, the Lamb of God. He was broken for us. His body was wrapped in white linen and hidden in a tomb for three days. The one that finds Him receives the reward of the new birth!

VII. How Should Believers Celebrate the Passover?

If you have ever read over a Passover Seder, the rabbis have expanded it well beyond the instructions given by Moses. There can be many wonderful spiritual lessons drawn from all items of the Passover, from the bitter herbs (of bondage) to the sweet fruits (of salvation). If the Holy Spirit leads you to observe the Passover in this way, I would strongly suggest that you leave out the egg. The egg is a symbol of Semiramis and was added after Babylon.

There is a saying among the rabbis that "Messiah will settle all things." It can also be quoted "Messiah will interpret all things." It gives us the understanding that Messiah will help us understand the things of God is complete clarity. I believe that He has done this with the Passover:

The Feasts of the LORD Study Guide | DVD

Matthew 26:26-30 (NKJV)
[26] And as they were eating, Jesus took bread, blessed and broke *it,* and gave *it* to the disciples and said, "Take, eat; this is My body." [27] Then He took the cup, and gave thanks, and gave *it* to them, saying, "Drink from it, all of you. [28] For this is My blood of the new covenant, which is shed for many for the remission of sins. [29] But I say to you, I will not drink of this fruit of the vine from now on until that day when I drink it new with you in My Father's kingdom." [30] And when they had sung a hymn, they went out to the Mount of Olives.

I believe that Jesus interpreted the Passover and reduced the elements of it down to bread and wine. A Believer's Passover Seder would include:

- Telling the great story of the Gospel - how Jesus came and gave His life for us. Use unleavened bread to show how it represents Jesus (also take communion with it).
- A time of contemplation to insure we have His blood over every doorpost in our lives and that we have received everything His sacrifice has done for us.
- Celebrating Communion.
- Praise and Worship.

Review Questions

1. What three feasts comprise the Spring Feasts?

The Feasts of the LORD Study Guide | DVD

---

2. How many prophetic promises were fulfilled during Passover week?

---

3. What day and time did Jesus die on the Cross for us?

---

4. When did Jesus raise from the dead?

5. How does unleavened bread represent Jesus?

6. What did Jesus reduce Passover to?

The Feasts of the LORD Study Guide | DVD

Lesson Five

The Spring Feasts - Part 2

In our last lesson, we looked at the first of the Spring Feasts: Passover. In this lesson, we will be looking at the Feast of Unleavened Bread and First Fruits.

I. The Feast of Unleavened Bread

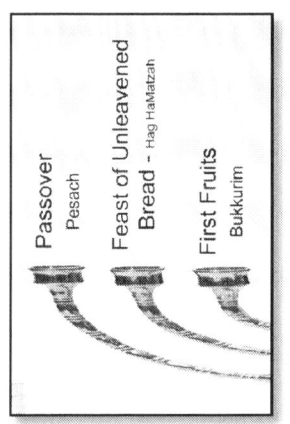

Exodus 12:30-34 (NKJV)
[30] So Pharaoh rose in the night, he, all his servants, and all the Egyptians; and there was a great cry in Egypt, for *there was* not a house where *there was* not one dead. [31] Then he called for Moses and Aaron by night, and said, "Rise, go out from among my people, both you and the children of Israel. And go, serve the Lord as you have said. [32] Also take your flocks and your herds, as you have said, and be gone; and bless me also." [33] And the Egyptians urged the people, that they might send them out of the land in haste. For they said, "We *shall* all *be* dead." [34] So the people took their dough before it was leavened, having their kneading bowls bound up in their clothes on their shoulders.

Exodus 12:37-39 (NKJV)
[37] Then the children of Israel journeyed from Rameses to Succoth, about six hundred thousand men on foot, besides children. [38] A mixed multitude went up with them also, and flocks and herds--a great deal of livestock. [39] And they

baked unleavened cakes of the dough which they had brought out of Egypt; for it was not leavened, because they were driven out of Egypt and could not wait, nor had they prepared provisions for themselves.

In the exodus from Egypt, the children of Israel did not have time to allow their dough to rise before leaving. This was planned by God to provide a memorial feast that would both point to Jesus and the life of the believer.

Exodus 12:16-17 (NKJV)
[16] On the first day *there shall be* a holy convocation, and on the seventh day there shall be a holy convocation for you. No manner of work shall be done on them; but *that* which everyone must eat--that only may be prepared by you. [17] So you shall observe *the Feast of* Unleavened Bread, for on this same day I will have brought your armies out of the land of Egypt. Therefore you shall observe this day throughout your generations as an everlasting ordinance.

II. Jesus & the Feast of Unleavened Bread

John 6:1-4 (NKJV)
[1] After these things Jesus went over the Sea of Galilee, which is *the Sea* of Tiberias. [2] Then a great multitude followed Him, because they saw His signs which He performed on those who were diseased. [3] And Jesus went up on the mountain, and there He sat with His disciples. [4] Now the Passover, a feast of the Jews, was near.

This is the backdrop for Jesus feeding the five thousand in John 6. As a nation, Israel was approaching the Feast of Unleavened Bread. This great multitude of people was following Him to hear the Word of God and to have their bodies healed by Messiah's touch. Jesus knew that He was getting ready to cross over to Capernaum and did not want to send the people away hungry, as they would all have a long journey ahead of them.

He feeds the five thousand with five loaves and two small fish (a small boy's lunch), then sends his disciples on to Capernaum by boat. A storm suddenly comes up, and we have the story of Jesus walking on the water and saving His disciples.

The next day, the people followed Jesus to Capernaum. They came for physical food and not spiritual food. Jesus has to change their thinking. They were so wrapped up in the physical that they were missing the spiritual significance of what was going on, especially in relation to the Spring Feasts!

> **John 6:25-31 (NKJV)**
> [25] And when they found Him on the other side of the sea, they said to Him, "Rabbi, when did You come here?" [26] Jesus answered them and said, "Most assuredly, <u>I say to you, you seek Me, not because you saw the signs, but because you ate of the loaves and were filled.</u> [27] Do not labor for the food which perishes, but for the food which endures to everlasting life, which the Son of Man will give you, because God the Father has set His seal on Him." [28] Then they said to Him, "What shall we do, that we may work the works of God?" [29] Jesus answered and said to them, "This is the work of God, that you believe in Him whom He sent." [30] Therefore they said to Him, "What sign will You perform then, that we may see it and believe You? What work will You do? [31] <u>Our fathers ate the manna in the desert; as it is written, *'He gave them bread from heaven to eat.'*</u> "

When everyone showed up looking for Jesus, He knew that they were missing the point of the miracles of the loaves and fishes. Jesus rebuked them and tried to direct them to the spiritual aspect of what He was trying to teach them. They still did not get it. They said "teach us how to do the works of God too" referring to multiplying the food. Jesus tried to refocus them by telling them "Here it is guys, believe in Me!" Their response was to bring up Moses. Since Messiah was to come like Moses, they tried to force Him to teach them to multiply food. Finally Jesus told them directly what He was trying to teach them:

> **John 6:32-36 (NKJV)**
> [32] Then Jesus said to them, "Most assuredly, I say to you, Moses did not give you the bread from heaven, <u>but My Father gives you the true bread from heaven</u>. [33] For the bread of God is He who comes down from heaven and gives life to the world." [34] Then they said to Him, "Lord, give us this bread always." [35] And Jesus said to them, "<u>I am the bread of life. He who comes to Me shall never hunger, and he who believes in Me shall never thirst.</u> [36] But I said to you that you have seen Me and yet do not believe.

Jesus is the unleavened bread of the Father come down from Heaven. He is the true bread of life.

III. The Power of the Feast of Unleavened Bread

a. The Two Sabbaths and Seven Days

The Feast of Unleavened Bread starts and ends with a Sabbath. This is to teach us that salvation and sanctification are works of God and not man. Jesus is the author and finisher of our faith (Heb 12:2). Seven signifies God's plan of salvation.

b. Getting the Leaven Out

Leaven in the Old Testament became a type and shadow of sin, Egypt and the things of this carnal world. Jesus was the only one that came into this world without leaven (sin). He came as the perfect sacrifice (without sin) that could purchase our redemption.

We must follow the example of Jesus and remove the leaven of this world from our lives. Unleavened bread is used to illustrate consecration and separation in the life of the believer. We are to live a life that has been separated from the world and to God's purposes in the earth.

We must allow the Holy Spirit to purge sin and worldliness from our lives. It is His work, and we must not grieve Him by resisting His working in us.

IV. Ways Believers Can Celebrate Unleavened Bread

In a traditional Jewish home, the family will make sure that the home is completely cleaned and that there is no possibility of any leaven remaining in the home. This massive cleaning of Jewish homes in preparation for Unleavened Bread is where we get the tradition of "Spring Cleaning." If a Jewish man owns a bakery, he will sell it to a gentile friend for one penny during the feast and purchase it back for one penny after the feast is completed.

The Feasts of the LORD Study Guide | DVD

A traditional Jewish family will only eat unleavened bread during the entire Spring Feasts. It is a time of reminding them of how they came out of Egypt in haste.

Now for Believers in Messiah

The first year that my family celebrated the Spring Feasts, we ate only unleavened bread for several days. By the third day of the feast, the Holy Spirit began dealing with us that we, like the people in John 6, were missing the point. Jesus is the unleavened bread, so we now see its fulfillment in Him. We must learn from that fulfillment and bring true spiritual application to our lives. Here are several suggestions:

   a.   **Search Your Heart for Leaven**

   Leaven represents sin and worldliness. Has sin and worldliness crept into your life like leaven? Before the invention of the yeast packets that we buy in the store to make bread, the dough was set out and exposed to the world long enough for the fermenting process to begin naturally. In other words, the leavening process is natural when the dough is exposed long enough to the world.

   Our constant exposure to the world and its systems allows small deposits of spiritual leaven into our hearts and minds. As long as we are in this world, the leaven of this world will constantly try to gain a foothold in our lives. The cure is threefold:

   - Examination
   - Repentance
   - The Blood of the Lamb

We need to spend extra time during Unleavened Bread to allow the Holy Spirit to show us what leaven of the world has infected our lives. Unchecked, it will continue until it has infected our entire being. Isn't the Lord gracious in giving us the feasts? It is a yearly time of examination before the world gets too strong of a foothold in our lives!

b. Fasting the Leaven

One of the major ways the leaven of this world gets into our lives is through the secular media. Many have fasted all secular television, movies and radio during the feast. It also allows them more time to listen to the Holy Spirit as they work the leaven out of their lives.

V. First Fruits

Leviticus 23:9-11 (NKJV)
^{9} And the Lord spoke to Moses, saying, ^{10} "Speak to the children of Israel, and say to them: 'When you come into the land which I give to you, and reap its harvest, then you shall bring a sheaf of the firstfruits of your harvest to the priest. ^{11} He shall wave the sheaf before the Lord, to be accepted on your behalf; on the day after the Sabbath the priest shall wave it.

Sunday morning after the Sabbath, the High Priest would wave the first sheaf of Barley that was harvested. It was a testimony that God would bring the full harvest

As the High Priest was waving the sheaf of Barley before the LORD when Jesus gave His life for us, Jesus was appearing before the

The Feasts of the LORD Study Guide | DVD

Father as the first fruits of salvation. Jesus is the fulfillment of First Fruits. He is:

- The firstborn of the Father (Heb 1:6).
- The firstborn of every creature (Col 1:15)
- The firstborn of Mary (Matt 1:23-25)
- The firstborn from the dead (Rev 1:5)
- The firstborn of many brethren (Rom 8:29)

Review Questions

1. How did Jesus fulfill the Feast of Unleavened Bread?

2. As believers, how are some of the ways we can enter into the Feast of Unleavened Bread?

3. What is the significance of First Fruits?

The Feasts of the LORD Study Guide | DVD

Lesson Six

The Summer Feast

Leviticus 23:15-17 (NKJV)
[15] 'And you shall count for yourselves from the day after the Sabbath, from the day that you brought the sheaf of the wave offering: seven Sabbaths shall be completed. [16] Count fifty days to the day after the seventh Sabbath; then you shall offer a new grain offering to the Lord. [17] You shall bring from your dwellings two wave *loaves* of two-tenths *of an ephah.* They shall be of fine flour; they shall be baked with leaven. *They are* the firstfruits to the Lord.

We will now examine the Summer Feast. I believe this feast speaks to where we are prophetically in God's timetable for the redemption of all mankind. To better understand this powerful feast, let's take a look at the purpose of the Feast of Weeks.

Names for This Feast

- Feast of Weeks (seven weeks of counting)
- Shavuot
- Pentecost (is a Greek word meaning fifty)
- Latter Fruits (the wheat harvest)
- Day of the Congregation (Deut 18:16)

Biblical Life Publishing

The Feasts of the LORD Study Guide | DVD

Historical and Prophetic Insights into This Feast

Shavuot is a remembering/divine rehearsal of God giving the Torah to His people. Moses descended from the mountain of fire (Mount Sinai) with the Ten Commandments written on two stone tablets. (I want to note that the Ten Commandments, which is a condensed summary of Torah, were given on two tablets. We will touch on this in a few moments.)

It is a celebration to reawaken and strengthen personal relationships with God by rededication to the observance and study of Torah - the most precious heritage.[13]

At the original Shavuot, the children of Israel came to Mount Sinai (a mountain in which the fire of God burned brightly). The writer of the Book of Hebrews tells us about this event:

---

[13] Sampson, Robin & Pierce, Linda. Biblical Feasts: A Family Guide to the Biblical Feasts. Heart of Wisdom Publishing, Woodbridge, VA Copyright © 1997. Spring Feasts - page 129.

Hebrews 12:18-21 (NKJV)
[18] For you have not come to the mountain that may be touched and that burned with fire, and to blackness and darkness and tempest, [19] and the sound of a trumpet and the voice of words, so that those who heard *it* begged that the word should not be spoken to them anymore. [20] (For they could not endure what was commanded: *"And if so much as a beast touches the mountain, it shall be stoned or shot with an arrow."* [21] And so terrifying was the sight *that* Moses said, *"I am exceedingly afraid and trembling."*)

In Hebrews, the writer is contrasting Mount Zion with Mount Sinai. The power of God was strong and shook the entire mountain as God's fire burned upon it, and God's Torah came from it. It was so powerful that even Moses was trembling with holy fear.

We then need to contrast that day with the day of Pentecost after the resurrection of Jesus.

Acts 2:1-4 (NKJV)
[1] When the Day of Pentecost had fully come, they were all with one accord in one place.
[2] And suddenly there came a sound from heaven, as of a rushing mighty wind, and it filled the whole house where they were sitting. [3] Then there appeared to them divided tongues, as of fire, and *one* sat upon each of them. [4] And they were all filled with the Holy Spirit and began to speak with other tongues, as the Spirit gave them utterance.

We now realize that the fire on Mount Sinai was the presence of the Holy Spirit. On the Day of Pentecost, the fire from the mountain moved into the hearts of those that embraced Messiah. There is a twofold purpose for this:

> **Witness**: The Torah was a witness in the earth that there was indeed one true God and this God, the God of Abraham, Isaac and Jacob, had given His instruction into the earth as a witness of who He is and what He expects of mankind. Mount Sinai displayed His power through the fire that was upon it. Today, His people display His power through the fire that is in them!
>
> Jesus is the living Torah - He is Almighty God come in the flesh to fulfill (to make full and understood) His Torah. You cannot separate Jesus from the Word.

Fire: The fire of God that was on the mountain has now descended into the hearts of men. The fire represents the power of God to do two things:

- Testify of who Jesus really is and what He has accomplished.
- The power to live the Torah that was given on the first Pentecost!

We will need this fire in the days ahead!

Hebrews 12:22-29 (NKJV)
22 But you have come to Mount Zion and to the city of the living God, the heavenly Jerusalem, to an innumerable company of angels, 23 to the general assembly and church of the firstborn *who are* registered in heaven, to God the Judge of all, to the spirits of just men made perfect, 24 to Jesus the Mediator of the new covenant, and to the blood of sprinkling that speaks better things than *that of* Abel. 25 See that you do not refuse Him who speaks. For if they did not escape who refused Him who spoke on earth, much more *shall we not escape* if we turn away from Him who *speaks* from heaven, 26 whose voice then shook the earth; but now He has promised, saying, *"Yet once more I shake not only the earth, but also heaven."* 27 Now this, *"Yet once more,"* indicates the removal of those things that are being shaken, as of things that are made, that the things which cannot be shaken may remain. 28 Therefore, since we are receiving a kingdom which cannot be shaken, let us have grace, by which we may serve God acceptably with reverence and godly fear. 29 For our God *is* a consuming fire.

As we approach the end of days, God is speaking powerfully again. His people are warned not to refuse Him as He speaks. He will speak through the shaking that will not only shake the earth, but also heaven. As we approach the prophetic fulfillment of the Fall Feasts, God is going to begin realigning His people with His purposes. He will also begin to judge things in the earth. It will not be like the last two thousand years. It will begin with an "Old Testament" flavor to it. God will continue to convict of sin to save souls and heal broken bodies, but He will also move quickly to judge unrighteousness and to overthrow satanic strongholds.

Understanding the Fire of God

The fire of God is as Hebrews 12:29 says - "a consuming fire." Let's take a look at three purposes of His holy fire.

His Fire In Us	His Fire Through Us	His Fire in the World
Burns out the sin in our lives and burns a hedge of protection around us.	Provides a powerful witness through signs & wonders of who Jesus really is.	Judges & destroys satanic strongholds - spiritual, political & physical.

Two Loaves and Two Tablets

Shavuot marked the end of the Passover season. It was also a transition between two harvest times - the barley harvest and the wheat harvest. As I shared in the last lesson, barley represented the Jewish people and wheat represented the Gentiles. On the Day of Pentecost, there were two loaves represented before Almighty God in the Temple. One loaf was made of barley, and the other was made of wheat.

If you will remember, earlier in this lesson, I said another name for Shavuot was "The Day of Congregation." The wave offering of both loaves of bread represents that God's congregation (or harvest) will be made up of both Jew and Gentile. Messiah will hold them up together before the Father as one people gathered from all the nations of the earth!

Is it not interesting that another mini-Pentecost happened in the house of a Gentile? This mini-Pentecost proved to the early Messianic Jewish leaders that Gentiles were going to be added to Messiah and to the congregation of Israel.

Acts 10:44-48 (NKJV)
⁴⁴ While Peter was still speaking these words, the Holy Spirit fell upon all those who heard the word. ⁴⁵ And those of the circumcision who believed were astonished, as many as came with Peter, because the gift of the Holy Spirit had been poured out on the Gentiles also. ⁴⁶ For they heard them speak with tongues and magnify God. Then Peter answered, ⁴⁷ "Can anyone forbid water, that these should not be baptized who have received the Holy Spirit just as we *have?*" ⁴⁸ And he commanded them to be baptized in the name of the Lord. Then they asked him to stay a few days.

The Two Tablets of Stone

With God, nothing is by accident. Why were there two stone tablets that held the Ten Commandments? There are several very valid teachings on this:

The Vassal Nation: When a great king would conquer a smaller nation, he would write the agreement between himself and that vassal nation on two separate documents. One would be kept by the people and one would be kept by the king. Some believe that the two tablets of the Ten Commandments conform to this ancient practice.

Divine & Human: The Ten Commandments can be divided into two groups - how to walk with God and how to walk fairly with man. Thus, the first tablet contained the first five - how to walk with Almighty God, and the second tablet contained the last five - how to walk with others.

Loaves & Tablets: It is no accident that two loaves are waved before the LORD on Shavuot and two tablets of stone were given in its origin. It is possible that the two tablets represent the same thing the two loaves do: that Jew and Gentile would come to God through one that was like Moses. Both would walk according to the Laws of God through the power and completed work of Messiah! This is becoming more evident as we approach the end of days, so we need to heed Hebrews 12 and hear what God is saying to the Church!

Review Questions

1. What are the different names given for the Summer Feast?

2. What is this feast supposed to reawaken and strengthen in us?

The Feasts of the LORD Study Guide | DVD

3. What is the contrast between the first Pentecost and the one we read about in Acts 2?

First Pentecost	Acts 2 Pentecost

4. There are three aspects of the fire of God given in this lesson. What are they?

5. What do the two loaves that are waved before the LORD represent?

The Feasts of the LORD Study Guide | DVD

6. What warning can the Church take from Hebrews 12 as we approach the end of days?

The Feasts of the LORD Study Guide | DVD

Lesson Seven
The Fall Feasts - Part 1

As I begin teaching on the Fall Feasts, I want to do so cautiously because I will begin dealing with prophetic images that have not yet been fulfilled. I answered the call to ministry thirty-six years ago. I have seen many teachers of prophecy present their views with absolute resolve accompanied with harsh words for anyone that disagreed. Yet time and time again, many of their conclusions were proved to be incorrect.

One of the most blatant mistakes of main stream evangelical prophecy teachers was seen in 1948. A large majority believed that the Church had replaced Israel (i.e. Replacement Theology) and that Israel would never become a nation again or at least until the physical return of Jesus. The few ministers that dared to teach that Israel would become a nation (and probably overnight) were scorned and called "heretics." Yet in 1948, Israel did become a nation again, and all those scorning ministers took thousands of their books out of print because they were all wrong!

I have also been told by several individuals (who in the past have worked for some of our current teachers of prophecy) that the ministries had warehouses full of books that they could no longer sell. They could not sell them because (as the prophetic work of God unfolded) their theories were found to be incorrect.

I believe today we are facing the same situation. Almost every evangelical prophecy teacher has dismissed the importance of Torah and the Feasts of the LORD. Thanks to Constantine and anti-Semitism in the Early Church, the Body of Christ was disenfranchised from the very foundations of our faith. The result was that we have been brought to conclusions prophetically that were not based on the patterns established by the Almighty. Just as the Jews in the New Testament period missed who Jesus was (because of their preconceived ideas that only took portions of God's prophetic picture), we are in danger of doing the same thing. The Apostle Paul reminds us:

> **1 Corinthians 13:8-12 (NKJV)**
> [8] Love never fails. But whether *there are* prophecies, they will fail; whether *there are* tongues, they will cease; whether *there is* knowledge, it will vanish away. [9] For we know in part and we prophesy in part. [10] But when that which is perfect has come, then that which is in part will be done away. [11] When I was a child, I spoke as a child, I understood as a child, I thought as a child; but when I became a man, I put away childish things. [12] For now we see in a mirror, dimly, but then face to face. Now I know in part, but then I shall know just as I also am known.

Some teach that this scripture was fulfilled when the New Testament was completed. This position is not taken regarding prophecy, but rather as opposition against tongues. They fail to see that knowledge has not vanished. I believe that Paul was extremely sensitive to the fact that many of his brethren had rejected Jesus because God had not fulfilled prophecy the way that they demanded. He realized that after prophecy has been fulfilled, God's plan can be clearly seen. In prophecy, as well as life, hindsight is always 20/20. Therefore, we are looking through the glass of prophetic scripture in a dim light. More understanding of scripture and events, both hidden and unfolding, is being revealed more quickly than ever before. We must stay sensitive to the Holy Spirit and stay informed as to what He is revealing to properly understand the days that are ahead of us.

I. Between The Feast of Shavuot and the Day of Trumpets

The Length of Time Between Shavuot and Trumpets

There is a long, hard summer between the Feast of Shavuot and the Day of Trumpets. This long period is symbolic of the long period between the formation of the Church at the Feast of Weeks and the regathering of Israel to the trumpet blast calling all born again believers.[14]

Tisha B'Av

Tisha B'Av is a time of mourning and fasting for the Jewish people. The fast commemorates the destruction of the First and Second Temples in Jerusalem, which occurred about 656 years apart, but on the same date.[15]

What is interesting is that the 9th of Av has another important event. It was the date when the Children of Israel refused to cross into the Promised Land. This caused

---

[14] Sampson, Robin & Pierce, Linda. Biblical Feasts: A Family Guide to the Biblical Feasts. Heart of Wisdom Publishing, Woodbridge, VA Copyright © 1997. Fall Feasts, Page 3.
[15] Wikipedia. http://en.wikipedia.org/wiki/Tisha_B'Av#cite_note-0

the people of God to wander 40 years in the wilderness until that generation died out. It is believed that Israel, as a people, never repented of their disobedience. The result is that there is an open window to the enemy to attack them during this period each year.

Teshuvah

Teshuvah (meaning return or repent) is a forty day period that begins on Elul 1 and ends on the Day of Atonement. This is a time to examine one's life and to restore one's relationship with both God and man. It is interesting to note that this time falls between the two feasts. It is the work of the Gospel to call men to repentance and to return to God.

The Number Forty

The number forty has long been universally recognized as an important number, both on account of the frequency of its occurrence, and the uniformity of its association with a period of probation, trial, and chastisement—(not judgment, like the number 9, which stands in connection with the punishment of enemies, but the chastisement of sons, and of a covenant people). It is the product of 5 and 8, and points to the action of grace (5), leading to and ending in revival and renewal (8). This is certainly the case where Forty relates to a period of evident probation. But where it relates to enlarged dominion, or to renewed or extended rule, then it does so in virtue of its factors 4 and 10, and in harmony with their signification.[16]

II. The Day of Trumpets

Leviticus 23:23-25 (NKJV)
[23] Then the Lord spoke to Moses, saying, [24] "Speak to the children of Israel, saying: 'In the seventh month, on the first *day* of the month, you shall have a sabbath-*rest,* a memorial of blowing of trumpets, a holy convocation. [25] You shall do no customary work *on it;* and you shall offer an offering made by fire to the Lord.' "

The first thing that I want you to notice is that I did not call this feast "Rosh Hashanah." This means "the head of the year." Biblically this feast is not the head of the year. The Almighty established the head of the year in the Spring before Passover. Many believe that the Jewish people picked up this concept while they were in Babylon. This time of year was the Babylonian New Year, which we completely reject. Almighty God calls this feast "Yom T'Ruah" -- so we will stick with the Word of God.

There are Jewish idioms associated with this feast. Yom T'Ruah begins at the first of the month (or on a new moon). Remember in session one, we dealt with Rosh Hodesh (the head of the month)? Because it could fall within a two-day period

---

[16] Bible Numbers. http://www.biblestudy.org/bibleref/meaning-of-numbers-in-bible/40.html

and could be complicated by a cloudy night, "no man would know the day or hour." This is directly connected to the Lord's return:

> **Matthew 24:36 (NKJV)**
> [36] "But of that day and hour no one knows, not even the angels of heaven, but My Father only.

By using this Jewish idiom, Jesus has connected His return with Yom T'Ruah.

Yom T'Ruah is a call from Heaven that God is going to be making announcements. It is a time that Heaven speaks. Those that are sensitive to the Holy Spirit will find that He speaks clearly during this time period. Many times, God will begin giving His people insights to prepare them for the next year. God has promised us that:

> **Amos 3:7 (NKJV)**
> [7] Surely the Lord God does nothing, Unless He reveals His secret to His servants the prophets.

God, in His graciousness, will always tell us things ahead of time so that we can prepare. It is my opinion that He will speak before the beginning of a year to help us prepare and be ready to move.

Themes Associated with the Day of Trumpets

1. Kingship
2. Marriage
3. Resurrection

This can be seen in three distinct blasts of the shofar at Trumpets:

1. Tekiah -- one long, straight blast (Kingship)

2.	Shevarim -- three medium, wailing sounds (Marriage)
3.	Teruah -- 10 quick blasts in short succession (Resurrection)

Kingship

We are rehearsing the day that Jesus will exert His Kingship upon the earth and men will have to answer for their actions.

Revelation 8:1-6 (NKJV)
¹ When He opened the seventh seal, there was silence in heaven for about half an hour. ² And I saw the seven angels who stand before God, and to them were given seven trumpets. ³ Then another angel, having a golden censer, came and stood at the altar. He was given much incense, that he should offer *it* with the prayers of all the saints upon the golden altar which was before the throne. ⁴ And the smoke of the incense, with the prayers of the saints, ascended before God from the angel's hand. ⁵ Then the angel took the censer, filled it with fire from the altar, and threw *it* to the earth. And there were noises, thunderings, lightnings, and an earthquake. ⁶ So the seven angels who had the seven trumpets prepared themselves to sound.

I believe that there is a progression in the Book of Revelation. We see certain things happening in the earth as Jesus (the King) begins to take the seven seals off the scroll. Only He was found worthy to remove them. Many believe that these seals represent Satan's authority on the earth. As Jesus begins stripping away Satan's authority, Satan begins releasing his anger upon the earth. We find in Revelation 11:15-19:

> **Revelation 11:15-19 (NKJV)**
> [15] Then the seventh angel sounded: And there were loud voices in heaven, saying, <u>"The kingdoms of this world have become *the kingdoms* of our Lord and of His Christ, and He shall reign forever and ever!"</u> [16] And the twenty-four elders who sat before God on their thrones fell on their faces and worshiped God, [17] saying: "We give You thanks, O Lord God Almighty, The One who is and who was and who is to come, <u>Because You have taken Your great power and reigned.</u> [18] The nations were angry, and <u>Your wrath has come,</u> And the time of the dead, that they should be judged, And that You should reward Your servants the prophets and the saints, And those who fear Your name, small and great, And should destroy those who destroy the earth." [19] Then the temple of God was opened in heaven, and the ark of His covenant was seen in His temple. And there were lightnings, noises, thunderings, an earthquake, and great hail.

This is the last trump that the Apostle Paul spoke of:

> **1 Corinthians 15:50-54 (NKJV)**
> [50] Now this I say, brethren, that flesh and blood cannot inherit the kingdom of God; nor does corruption inherit incorruption. [51] Behold, I tell you a mystery: We shall not all sleep, but we shall all be changed-- [52] in a moment, in the twinkling of an eye, <u>at the last trumpet. For the trumpet</u>

> will sound, and the dead will be raised incorruptible, and we shall be changed. [53] For this corruptible must put on incorruption, and this mortal *must* put on immortality. [54] So when this corruptible has put on incorruption, and this mortal has put on immortality, then shall be brought to pass the saying that is written: *"Death is swallowed up in victory."*

The last trump is also connected to the bowls of God's wrath upon the earth.

> **Revelation 16:1 (NKJV)**
> [1] Then I heard a loud voice from the temple saying to the seven angels, "Go and pour out the bowls of the wrath of God on the earth."

Marriage

As Babylon is being judged by the bowls of God's wrath, something else is going on in Heaven. Yom T'Ruah is also a call for the Wedding Feast!

> **Revelation 19:5-9 (NKJV)**
> [5] Then a voice came from the throne, saying, "Praise our God, all you His servants and those who fear Him, both small and great!" [6] And I heard, as it were, the voice of a great multitude, as the sound of many waters and as the sound of mighty thunderings, saying, "Alleluia! For the Lord God Omnipotent reigns! [7] Let us be glad and rejoice and give Him glory, for the marriage of the Lamb has come, and His wife has made herself ready." [8] And to her it was granted to be arrayed in fine linen, clean and bright, for the fine linen is the righteous acts of the saints. [9] Then he said to me, "Write:

'Blessed *are* those who are called to the marriage supper of the Lamb!' " And he said to me, "These are the true sayings of God."

Resurrection

1 Thessalonians 4:16-18 (NKJV)
[16] For the Lord Himself will descend from heaven with a shout, with the voice of an archangel, and <u>with the trumpet of God</u>. And the dead in Christ will rise first. [17] Then we who are alive *and* remain shall be caught up together with them in the clouds to meet the Lord in the air. And thus we shall always be with the Lord. [18] Therefore comfort one another with these words.

Behold, I Stand at the Door and Knock

Revelation 3:20 (NKJV)
[20] Behold, I stand at the door and knock. If anyone hears My voice and opens the door, I will come in to him and dine with him, and he with Me.

The Feasts of the LORD Study Guide | DVD

Review Questions

1. What does Teshuvah teach us?

2. What is the Feast of Trumpets not Rosh Hashanah?

3. How is the phrase "no man knows the day or hour" connected to the Day of Trumpets?

The Feasts of the LORD Study Guide | DVD

4. What three themes are associated with the Day of Trumpets?

5. In looking at Revelation 3:20 and the marriage covenant, what is the major component that the Church has overlooked?

The Feasts of the LORD Study Guide | DVD

Lesson Eight
The Fall Feasts - Part 2

In this lesson, we will be examining the remaining Fall Feasts.

The Day of Atonement

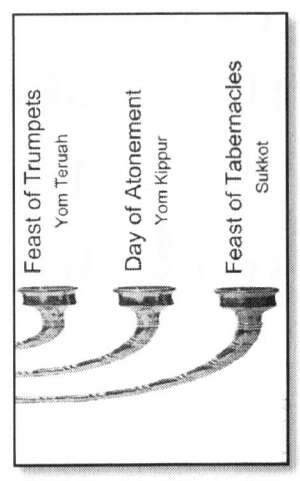

Leviticus 23:26-32 (NKJV)
26 And the Lord spoke to Moses, saying: 27 "Also the tenth *day* of this seventh month *shall be* the Day of Atonement. It shall be a holy convocation for you; you shall afflict your souls, and offer an offering made by fire to the Lord. 28 And you shall do no work on that same day, for it *is* the Day of Atonement, to make atonement for you before the Lord your God. 29 For any person who is not afflicted *in soul* on that same day shall be cut off from his people. 30 And any person who does any work on that same day, that person I will destroy from among his people. 31 You shall do no manner of work; *it shall be* a statute forever throughout your generations in all your dwellings. 32 It *shall be* to you a sabbath of *solemn* rest, and you shall afflict your souls; on the ninth *day* of the month at evening, from evening to evening, you shall celebrate your sabbath."

Biblical Life Publishing

The Feasts of the LORD Study Guide | DVD

I. Background on the Day of Atonement

This was the one day each year that the High Priest would go into the Holy of Holies to sprinkle the blood of a lamb on the right side of the Ark of the Covenant to make atonement for the sins of all the people of Israel.

This was the most solemn and holy day addressed in the Word of God. There is a warning with this day - if one does not afflict one's soul, he will be cut off from among the people.

The Two Goats

There were also two identical goats. One was "for God" and the other for "Azazel" (the scapegoat). The scapegoat carried the sins of the people into the desert and died.

II. Prophetic Significance

The Day of Atonement is a divine rehearsal of the "Day of the LORD." This is when Jesus returns to the earth, wars with the armies of darkness in the Valley of Armageddon, and then judges the nations. Everything that is not afflicted in soul before Him will be cut off.

Revelation 19:11-16 (NKJV)
[11] Now I saw heaven opened, and behold, a white horse. And He who sat on him *was* called Faithful and True, and in righteousness He judges and makes war. [12] His eyes *were* like a flame of fire, and on His head

The Feasts of the LORD Study Guide | DVD

were many crowns. He had a name written that no one knew except Himself. [13] He *was* clothed with a robe dipped in blood, and His name is called The Word of God. [14] And the armies in heaven, clothed in fine linen, white and clean, followed Him on white horses. [15] Now out of His mouth goes a sharp sword, that with it He should strike the nations. And He Himself will rule them with a rod of iron. He Himself treads the winepress of the fierceness and wrath of Almighty God. [16] And He has on *His* robe and on His thigh a name written: KING OF KINGS AND LORD OF LORDS.

III. Understanding "Afflicted" in Soul

Afflicted: Strongs #H6031 עָנָה `anah {aw-naw'} [17]
Meaning: 1) (Qal) to be occupied, be busied with 2) to afflict, oppress, humble, be afflicted, be bowed down 2a) (Qal) 2a1) to be put down, become low 2a2) to be depressed, be downcast 2a3) to be afflicted 2a4) to stoop 2b) (Niphal) 2b1) to humble oneself, bow down 2b2) to be afflicted, be humbled 2c) (Piel) 2c1) to humble, mishandle, afflict 2c2) to humble, be humiliated 2c3) to afflict 2d4) to humble, weaken oneself 2d) (Pual) 2d1) to be afflicted 2d2) to be humbled 2e) (Hiphil) to afflict 2f) (Hithpael) 2f1) to humble oneself 2f2) to be afflicted
Origin: a primitive root [possibly rather ident. with 06030 through the idea of looking down or browbeating]; TWOT - 1651,1652; v
Usage: AV - afflict 50, humble 11, force 5, exercised 2, sing 2, Leannoth 1, troubled 1, weakened 1, misc 11; 84

This, of all days, is a day to humble ourselves before God – for we are approaching the Judgment Bar of the Almighty!

---

[17] Strong's Enhanced Lexicon. BibleWorks for Windows 7.0. BibleWorks, LLC, Norfolk, VA. Copyright © 2006.

Biblical Life Publishing

IV. What It Teaches Us

When we look at the patterns of the feasts, we find:

Passover: The blood is shed to set us free from the powers of darkness.

Unleavened Bread: God enables us to walk in a level of holiness undreamed of since the Fall, because of the Blood of the Lamb.

First Fruits: The initial work that God has done in our hearts because of the sacrifice of the Passover is just the beginning. We know the full harvest will be wrought in us.

Pentecost: We are supernaturally empowered by God's Spirit to walk in the ways of God and to become His witnesses in the earth.

Trumpets: God begins calling us together to give an account of our lives since His work has begun in us.

The Days of Awe: Ten days to make things right with both God and man. Ten is the number for testimony, law and responsibility.

Atonement: We must give an account for the life we have lived and the things we have accomplished since we have experienced Passover.

The Feast of Tabernacles

Leviticus 23:33-34 (NKJV)
³³ Then the Lord spoke to Moses, saying, ³⁴ "Speak to the children of Israel, saying: 'The fifteenth day of this seventh month *shall be* the Feast of Tabernacles *for* seven days to the Lord.

I. An Overall Look at Tabernacles

God's Salvation Plan

The Feast of Tabernacles lasts for eight days. Seven days are as described in verse 34 and then (in verse 39) God adds an additional Sabbath, thus 8.

Seven is the number that illustrates God's salvation plan. It also represents completeness, spiritual and perfection.

When God completes His work of salvation with man, He will add an extra day of rest (which represents the New Birth or New Beginning).

Man is given six thousand years for his reign upon the earth. The seventh millennium is the millennial reign of Messiah. The eighth day represents the New Heavens and New Earth.

The Feasts of the LORD Study Guide | DVD

The Time of Jesus' Birth

Jesus was born during the Feasts of Tabernacles. Many believe He was born on the first day in a Sukkah (Manger) and was circumcised on the eighth day.

Lessons from the Lulav

Leviticus 23:40 (NKJV)
⁴⁰ And you shall take for yourselves on the first day the fruit of beautiful trees, branches of palm trees, the boughs of leafy trees, and willows of the brook; and you shall rejoice before the Lord your God for seven days.

The waving of the Lulav shows us the state of various members of the community of faith. All must acknowledge their need for God and His desire to Tabernacle with His people.

The Palm: The palm bears fruit (deeds) but is not fragrant (spiritual blessing). This is like a person who lives by the letter of the Law but does not have compassion or love for others.

The Myrtle: The myrtle only has fragrance; it can't bear fruit. This is like a person who is "so Heavenly minded that he is no earthly good." He may recite scripture, but he doesn't produce fruit.

The Willow: The willow can neither produce fruit nor fragrance. This is like a person who is intrigued by different doctrines but never produces fruit.

The Citron: The citron creates both fruit and fragrance. This is a like a faithful believer who lives a balanced life in wisdom before God and man. Believers should strive to be like the citron. [18]

1 Corinthians 3:9-15 (NKJV)
[9] For we are God's fellow workers; you are God's field, *you are* God's building. [10] According to the grace of God which was given to me, as a wise master builder I have laid the foundation, and another builds on it. But let each one take heed how he builds on it. [11] For no other foundation can anyone lay than that which is laid, which is Jesus Christ. [12] Now if anyone builds on this foundation *with* gold, silver, precious stones, wood, hay, straw, [13] each one's work will become clear; for the Day will declare it, because it will be revealed by fire; and the fire will test each one's work, of what sort it is. [14] If anyone's work which he has built on *it* endures, he will receive a reward. [15] If anyone's work is burned, he will suffer loss; but he himself will be saved, yet so as through fire.

All mankind will be judged.

For those that have been redeemed by the Blood of the Lamb - our works will be judged.
For those that have rejected the gospel - their lives and sin will be judged.

---

[18] Scarlata, Robin & Pierce, Linda. A Family Guide to Biblical Holidays – Section Three: Fall Feasts. Heart of Wisdom Publications, Woodbridge, VA. Copyright 1999. Pages 83-84.

II. The Millennial Reign

Revelation 20:1-6 (NKJV)
[1] Then I saw an angel coming down from heaven, having the key to the bottomless pit and a great chain in his hand. [2] He laid hold of the dragon, that serpent of old, who is *the* Devil and Satan, and bound him for a thousand years; [3] and he cast him into the bottomless pit, and shut him up, and set a seal on him, so that he should deceive the nations no more till the thousand years were finished. But after these things he must be released for a little while. [4] And I saw thrones, and they sat on them, and judgment was committed to them. Then *I saw* the souls of those who had been beheaded for their witness to Jesus and for the word of God, who had not worshiped the beast or his image, and had not received *his* mark on their foreheads or on their hands. And they lived and reigned with Christ for a thousand years. [5] But the rest of the dead did not live again until the thousand years were finished. This *is* the first resurrection. [6] Blessed and holy *is* he who has part in the first resurrection. Over such the second death has no power, but they shall be priests of God and of Christ, and shall reign with Him a thousand years.

III. Eighth Day - New Heaven and New Earth

Revelation 21:1-8 (NKJV)
[1] Now I saw a new heaven and a new earth, for the first heaven and the first earth had passed away. Also there was no more sea. [2] Then I, John, saw the holy city, New Jerusalem, coming down out of heaven from God, prepared as a bride adorned for her husband. [3] And I heard a loud voice from heaven saying, "Behold, the tabernacle of God *is* with men, and He will dwell with them, and they shall be His people. God Himself will be with them *and be* their God. [4] And God will wipe away every tear from their eyes; there shall be no more death, nor sorrow, nor crying. There shall be no more pain, for the former things have passed away." [5] Then He who sat on the throne said, "Behold, I make all things new." And He said to me, "Write, for these words are true and faithful." [6] And He said to me, "It is done! I am the Alpha and the Omega, the Beginning and the End. I will give of the fountain of the water of life freely to him who thirsts. [7] He who overcomes shall inherit all things, and I will be his God and he shall be My son. [8] But the cowardly, unbelieving, abominable, murderers, sexually immoral, sorcerers, idolaters, and all liars shall have their part in the lake which burns with fire and brimstone, which is the second death."

The Feasts of the LORD Study Guide | DVD

Review Questions

1. What does the Day of Atonement represent?

2. What does it mean to "afflict one's soul?"

3. What three events do we see in the Feast of Tabernacles?

4. What do the four branches of the Lulav teach us?

The Palm:

The Myrtle:

The Willow:

The Citron:

The Feasts of the LORD Study Guide | DVD

The Feasts of the LORD Study Guide | DVD

Lesson Nine
Hanukkah & Purim

There are two other feasts or holidays that are celebrated by the Jewish people that were not established in the Torah. These feasts do hold biblical, spiritual, historical, and prophetic significance - both for the Jewish people and for believers. In the final lesson in this series, we will be examining both Hanukkah and Purim.

I.   Hanukkah - The Feast of Dedication (Lights)

Have you ever wondered why many Jews in the Book of Acts had difficulty with understanding how Gentiles could become a part of Israel without physical circumcision? The zeal of the Pharisees from the School of Shammai regarding circumcision among the Gentile believers caused the Apostle Paul to write the Epistle of Galatians. There is some speculation as to the timing of the writing of the Book of Galatians. We find the following in the Introduction to the Book of Galatians in the New Spirit-Filled Life Study Bible:

> *The question of the date of Galatians hinges mainly on the correlation of 2:1-10 with Paul's visit to Jerusalem recorded in Acts. If the letter was written to believers in South Galatia, it was likely composed in the year A.D. 49, after Paul's first missionary journey but prior to the Jerusalem Council meeting recorded in Acts 15. Thus the event described in Galatians 2 refers to Acts 11:27-30 or some*

other unrecorded meeting. If the letter was written to believers in Northern Galatia, then it was written after the beginning of Paul's second missionary journey in A.D. 53-56 and after the Jerusalem Council of Acts 15. In this case, Galatians 2 likely refers to this Jerusalem Council, which had recently been convened. [19]

The sole purpose in writing the Epistle to the Galatians was to deal with the issue of establishing salvation by physical circumcision. Galatians is not an "anti-Torah" book. It is a letter written by the Apostle Paul to let the Gentile believers know that circumcision does not grant salvation, rather it is the faith in the completed work of Messiah. Through this new faith, the Almighty circumcises the hearts of the believers. This circumcision of the heart is a greater circumcision than that of the flesh!

As we study the events surrounding Hanukkah, we will begin to understand why circumcision was such a controversial subject in the Book of Acts and required a Council meeting in Jerusalem to settle the matter.

The History of Hanukkah

The Encyclopædia Britannica gives the following insights into the origin of Hanukkah:

> *Jewish festival that begins on Kislev 25 (in December, according to the Gregorian calendar) and is celebrated for eight days. Hanukkah reaffirms the ideals of Judaism and commemorates in particular the rededication of the Second Temple in Jerusalem by the lighting of candles on*

---

[19] Hayford, Jack W, Executive Editor. The New Spirit-Filled Life Bible, Thomas Nelson Publishers, Nashville, TN. Copyright 2002. Page 1628.

each day of the festival. Although not mentioned in the Hebrew Scriptures, Hanukkah came to be widely celebrated and remains one of the most popular Jewish religious observances.

According to I Maccabees, the celebration of Hanukkah was instituted by Judas Maccabeus in 165 BCE to celebrate his victory over Antiochus IV Epiphanes, the Seleucid king who had invaded Judaea, tried to Hellenize the Jews, and desecrated the Second Temple in Jerusalem. Following his victory in a three-year struggle against Antiochus, Judas ordered the cleansing and restoration of the Temple. After it was purified, a new altar was installed and dedicated on Kislev 25. Judas then proclaimed that the dedication of the restored Temple should be celebrated every year for eight days beginning on that date. In II Maccabees the celebration is compared to the festival of Sukkoth (the Feast of Tabernacles or Feast of Booths), which the Jews were unable to celebrate because of the invasion of Antiochus. Hanukkah, therefore, emerged as a celebration of the dedication, as the word itself suggests.[20]

There is much that the reference above leaves out of the story. When believers try to conduct their own research, they are not given the full story. No wonder most believers do not see any significance in this event that occurred during the Intertestamental Period. Here is some important information that you need to know:

---

[20] Encyclopædia Britannica 2009 Deluxe Edition Software. Copyright 2009 by Encyclopædia Britannica Inc.

1. Upon conquering Judea, Antiochus IV Epiphanes desecrated the Temple in Jerusalem with two acts:

- He erected a statue of Apollo in the Temple. (Although he placed his own face on the statue.)
- He sacrificed a hog on the sacred altar of God on the birthday of Apollo - December 25.

2. He demanded that the Jewish people abandon the Torah and embrace the Grecian culture.

- He made eating pork mandatory for all Jewish people. The flesh and blood of swine was sacred to pagan, sun-worshipping religions. Refusal to eat pork held the death penalty.
- He made circumcision illegal. The penalty for circumcising their male infants was death.

Although many complied with the Hellenization of Judea, many did not. Antiochus' response was extremely violent and without mercy.

The extreme cruelty of Antiochus caused the Maccabees to rise up and drive Antiochus and his army out of Judea. He was driven out three years later, nearly to the date he invaded.

The Maccabees ordered the cleansing of the Temple, and a new altar was constructed that was made from unhewn stones. The Temple was cleansed, and it was now ready for rededication.

They found only enough oil to keep the Menorah in the Temple lit for one day, and it would take eight days to prepare a new supply. To all their amazement, the Menorah continued to burn for eight days. This is known as the miracle of the lights. Thus Hanukkah is known as both the Feast of Dedication (when the Temple was rededicated to God) and the Feast of Lights (referring to the miracle of the oil).

Significance to the Believer

1.   If it had not been for the Maccabees, Jesus would never have been able to enter into the Temple and minister - it would have still been defiled.

2.   The Feast of Dedication teaches us that we must yearly rededicate our temples (our bodies and lives) to Almighty God. We must have the zeal of the Maccabees to drive out all influences of Hellenization and paganism in our lives.

3.   The Feast of Lights teaches us that we must keep the fire of the Holy Spirit burning brightly within us.

4.   Eight is the number of new beginnings. If we stumble and let the influences of Antiochus (i.e. Hellenization) into our lives, God will give us grace to drive it out and rededicate ourselves to Him!

5. Jesus was conceived of the Holy Spirit during the Feast of Lights and was born during Tabernacles. How appropriate that the Light of the World was conceived during the Feast of Lights! Hanukkah is the time of year to conceive new things into your spirit by the Holy Spirit.

Food for Thought

Several things stand out to me that I want to address:

1. Through the Hellenization of the Church, we are all celebrating Christmas instead of the Feast of Lights. Everyone is speaking of spiritual birth, when we should be spiritually conceiving. It leaves us out of sync with the Kingdom of God.

2. At the time of Jesus, the Pharisees at the School of Shammai would have been just as zealous about Gentiles not eating pork as they were about circumcision. Although there is a veiled reference to it in the determination by the Council in Jerusalem, it was not a main issue. One can only conclude that Gentiles had begun eating according to Leviticus 11. We also see Paul addressing this issue in 1 Timothy 4:

> **1 Timothy 4:1-5 (NKJV)**
> [1] Now the Spirit expressly says that in latter times some will depart from the faith, giving heed to deceiving spirits and doctrines of demons, [2] speaking lies in hypocrisy, having their own conscience seared with a hot iron, [3] forbidding to marry, *and <u>commanding</u> <u>to abstain from foods which God created to be received with thanksgiving</u>* by those who believe and know the truth. [4] For every creature of God *is* good, and nothing is to be refused if it is received with thanksgiving; [5] for it is sanctified by the word of God and prayer.

The Feasts of the LORD Study Guide | DVD

> **Food**: Strongs # **1033** βρῶμα broma {bro'-mah}
> Meaning: from the base of <G977> (bibrosko); *food* (literal or figurative), <u>especially (cerimonial) articles allowed or forbidden by the Jewish law</u> :- meat, victuals.[21]

This understanding is also found in the "Complete Word Study Dictionary":

> βρῶμα [See Stg: <G1033>]
> *bróma*; gen. *brómatos*, neut. noun from *bibróskō* <G977>, to eat. That which is chewed such as meat or vegetables in opposition to milk which is liquid (1 Cor. 3:2). Used with its primary meaning as food (Matt. 14:15; Mark 7:19; Luke 3:11; 9:13; 1 Cor. 6:13; Sept.: Gen. 6:21; 41:35ff.; Deut. 2:28; 2 Chr. 9:4). <u>Spoken of meats permitted by the Mosaic Law</u> (Heb. 9:10; 13:9); <u>of meats against which Jewish Christians observed certain scruples in eating</u> (Rom. 14:15, 20; 1 Cor. 8:8, 13; 1 Tim. 4:3). It denotes sustenance, nourishment (John 4:34) or that by which one lives. Used for spiritual food, manna, as an emblem of spiritual nourishment or instruction (1 Cor. 3:2; 10:3).[22]

This could just as easily been translated:

> "and commanding to abstain from Levitically approved foods which God created to be received with thanksgiving. . ."

---

[21] James Strong, *Strong's Talking Greek & Hebrew Dictionary*, (Austin, TX: WORDsearch Corp., 2007), WORDsearch CROSS e-book, Under: "1033"..

[22] Spiros Zodhiates, *The Complete Word Study Dictionary – New Testament*, (Chattanooga, TN: AMG Publishers, 1993), WORDsearch CROSS e-book, Under: "ß??μα".

This is further expressed by the Apostle Paul in verse 5, "for it is sanctified by the Word of God . . ." Sanctify means to separate for a purpose. The only place in the Word of God where God "separates" things for food is Leviticus 11.

II. Purim

The story of Purim is found in the Book of Esther. A young Jewish girl must hide her ancestry and is chosen to marry the King of Babylon. God uses this situation to save the Jewish people from being slaughtered by Haman. Mordecai reminds her that:

Esther 4:14 (NKJV)
¹⁴ For if you remain completely silent at this time, relief and deliverance will arise for the Jews from another place, but you and your father's house will perish. Yet who knows whether you have come to the kingdom for *such* a time as this?"

When Esther reveals her true Jewish lineage, God is able to save the Jewish people from certain destruction.

The story of Esther teaches us that one day the plans of the Anti-Christ will be overturned. Haman will also find his way into his own noose.

There may be a hint of prophetic insight in the story of Purim. Will the Body of Christ one day reveal its Jewish or Hebraic heritage and be used to save the Jewish people from the plans of the Anti-Christ before the returning of the LORD?

The Feasts of the LORD Study Guide | DVD

Review Questions

1. Why was the Epistle to the Galatians written?

2. What did Antioch IV Epiphanes do that has so heinous to the Jewish people?

3. What five things does Hanukkah teach believers today?

5. How can the story of Esther be connected to the Tribulation Period?

The Feasts of the LORD Study Guide | DVD

 # Recommended Reading

Biblical Feasts: A Family Guide to the Biblical Feasts by Robin Sampson & Linda Pierce. Heart of Wisdom Publishing, Woodbridge, WA

God's Appointed Customs: A Messianic Jewish Guide to the Biblical Lifecycle and Lifestyle by Barney Kasdan. Messanic Jewish Publishers, Baltimore, MD

God's Appointed Times: A Practical Guide for Understanding and Celebrating the Biblical Holidays by Barney Kasdan. Messanic Jewish Publishers, Baltimore, MD

The Feasts of the LORD: God's Prophetic Calendar from Calvary to the Kingdom by Kevin Howard & Marvin Rosenthal. Thomas Nelson Publishers, Nashville, TN.

The Messianic Church Arising by Dr. Robert D. Heidler. Glory of Zion International Ministries, Denton, TX.

The Feasts of the LORD and Their Fulfillment in Messiah Yeshua by Dr. Bruce R. Booker. Createspace.com

Israel's Feasts and Their Fullness by Batya R. Wootten. Key of David Publishing, St. Cloud, FL.

Biblical Life Publishing

The Feasts of the LORD Study Guide | DVD

Jesus in the Feasts of Israel: Restoring the Spiritual Realities of the Feasts to the Church by Dr. Richard Booker. Destiny Image, Shippensburg, PA.

Additional Resources

Biblical Life has many additional resources for your spiritual growth and preparation for ministry.

Biblical Life College & Seminary

BLCS specializes in nontraditional theological education (at home study). For over 28 years, BLCS has been preparing men and women for ministry worldwide. Our programs are balanced with solid academic requirements and cutting-edge, real-world, biblical teaching. Our students are transformed by the power and Word of God as they prepare to transform the world! Complete information is available on-line at:

http://www.biblical-life.com

Biblical Life Publishing

BLP is the publishing arm of Biblical Life. We are continually adding new studies that are available to the Body of Christ that include both DVD and MP3 series with study guides. These powerful series are being used for personal growth, home fellowships and church study groups worldwide. Complete information is available on-line at:

http://www.biblical-life.net

Biblical Life Assembly

BLA is Dr. Lake's local congregation. All of the weekly messages are posted on the church's website in MP3 for free download. Our Digital Library maintains at least one full year of weekly messages and permanently maintains complete series. To download our free teachings, visit the Digital Library at our website:

http://www.biblicallifeassembly.org

Made in the USA
Charleston, SC
27 January 2010